Praise For IDEAL Leadership

In my experience, I've found that management and leadership are many times treated as interchangeable concepts. While someone might think they are an effective manager because they possess the necessary practical skills, the magic behind truly great leaders is centered around strong character. Gary's book captures this perfectly, laying out in-the-trenches perspective around key differences in the two and the qualities important for leadership. If you want to ignite your career, lead a team of significance, or are looking for inspiration, "Ideal Leadership" is a must read!

Lori Tyler - Vice President of Global Marketing for AccessData

I've known Gary for over 15 years. Gary is a man of integrity, committed to success-generating habits with complete sincerity...nothing halfway, fully genuine. In his new book, Gary shares the critical ingredients necessary for quality leadership and the controls and influences each of us to lead the best ways we can. This is a must read for those of us that want to improve our leadership skills and grow our people.

Dave Heuermann - FVP Mt West Region, HomeStreet Bank

My belief is that character and influence are the essence of Leadership. Gary Varnells' book on moving from a management roll to leadership by developing great character and influence is an excellent guide to achieve that leadership role.

Chris Widener – Author of "The Art of Influence"

I have had the pleasure of knowing Gary for more than 20-years, and find him one of the most inspiring men I have ever met. He has faced challenges and persevered, learning and growing through each of life's never-ending tests. What makes Gary special is his leadership. He has developed the vision to see solutions where others see dead-ends. Gary empowers everyone he touches to be a better person and to achieve their dreams, much like that great coach or star player who makes everyone around him a better player. He works hard, remains humble, and dreams bold. I know I am a better person because I have the honor to call Gary my friend.

Jody Weis – Director, Public Safety, North America for Accenture

I've been friends with Gary Varnell for 7 years and he has always demonstrated integrity and strong character. Integrity and character creates influence and these are keys to great leadership. In his book on leadership and influence, Gary explains how and what it takes to become a great leader. This book is a must read for leaders and future leaders.

Todd Stottelmyre – Speaker; Best Selling Author of "Relentless Success" and Three Time MLB World Series Champion.

I have had the privilege to lead sales teams and sales organizations for the past 30 years. One thing my experience has taught me is there is a big difference between management and leadership. The biggest misconception I have seen, is when someone is promoted they think they are automatically a leader. Leadership is earned over time through the character traits and caring you display consistently toward your team. Gary Varnell's book is a must read to see where you are on either the management or leadership scale. Gary's book will help you develop from a manager into a leader.

Fred "Chip" Kron – Vice President of sales Amerifirst Financial

I've known Gary Varnell for 44 years. Gary has always been a leader, in all that he does. Gary's book on leadership and influence is a must read for those who want to become a leader and those leaders that want to become a great leader.

Tony Lucky Winston - Founder, Digital Media

Champions have a vision of what will be - before it happens and success is not a matter of chance, it's a matter of choice. Gary Varnell is a master at leadership and managing your goals. His new book, "Ideal Leadership," will give you the roadmap showing you how to get there!

John Lang – President of Pinnacle Development

Gary Varnell's recent publication focused on leadership and influence is a great tool for the modern employee toolbox. It sheds light on multiple areas of leadership that, if taken to heart, can fill gaps for the newest hire up to the company founder. What sets his book apart from others based on leadership is the fact that he takes into consideration the qualities and successful tactics of multiple leaders spread across multiple industries, instead of just those of the author. As a Leadership Consultant, I will certainly add this to my recommended reading.

Russell Williamson - Performance Consultant/Project Manager at Ascend LLC; Former Staff Sergeant Special Operations Air Force Warfare Center

IDEAL LEADERSHIP:

TRANSFORMATIONAL LEADERSHIP THROUGH CHARACTER AND INFLUENCE

Gary Varnell

JONES MEDIA PUBLISHING

Jones Media Publishing
10645 N. Tatum Blvd. Ste. 200-166
Phoenix, AZ 85028
www.JonesMediaPublishing.com

Printed in the United States of America

ISBN: 978-1-945849-32-9 paperback

Contents

ACKNOWLEDGMENTS

First, I want to thank my wife Donna Lynn Varnell for her love and support. Without Donna's support, I would not have written this book. I also want to thank Donna for the time she took editing this book. Lastly, I want to thank Donna for helping me become a better version of myself every day.

Greg Provenzano, as one of my mentors and leadership examples, has been a driving influence to many of my leadership thoughts in this book. Thank you for your example and mentorship.

Thank you, Larry Raskin. Larry has been a driving influence on my views and perspectives on leadership. Larry has helped me in many ways with my thinking and perspectives on leadership and how to be a winner in life.

Russell Williamson, thank you for allowing me to interview you for this book. As a millennial leader and trainer, your perspective was very valuable for this book and for its readers.

Jody Weis, Thank you for allowing me to interview you and the leadership perspective you added to this book. You have had very high levels of leadership experience from the military, FBI and as the Superintendent of the Chicago Police department. To lead at these levels, you have earned a high degree of influence.

Thank you, Janice Weis, for helping me with editing the grammar and word choice of this book. You have helped the book become a better read.

Fred "Chip' Kron, Thank you for your time and allowing me to interview you on your perspective and experience with leadership. Your experience and perspective as a mortgage business owner and now a corporate mortgage executive, are very valuable to the readers of this book. Your leadership and influence are evidenced by how many people from your previous company joined you at the company you currently work. This is the power of influence

Dave Heuermann, thank you for sharing your time and leadership perspective. Learning about your perspective on leadership, shows why you have had great successes in your business pursuits and why people follow you when you start at a new company. This shows the power of influence you have built.

Lori Tyler, Thank you for allowing me to interview you for this leadership book. Having your perspective and philosophy on leadership is of huge value to the readers. You are a leader that utilizes many of the qualities of true leadership and influence. This influence is evidenced by how many of your team members followed you from your previous company to your current company.

Tony Lucky Winston, I want to thank you for taking time out of your busy schedule to allow me to interview you as an entrepreneur leader. Your leadership perspective and experience is very valuable to entrepreneurs and corporate business leaders alike. Your success creating and building your company and its team is a testament to your leadership abilities and influence.

Introduction

A huge key to life's success is building relationships and creating true leadership. To create life's success will take influence. Influence is one of the main topics of this book and the most important key to success in building personal and business relationships. By the end of this book, you will know what a person of influence is. You will know what it takes to become a person of influence. You will also understand the person you become by committing to certain standards and morals. It is the person you become by living a life of high standards, excellence, and positivity. The keys to influence and the person you need to be are available to everyone. This success is something that everyone can accomplish. I want to note that by becoming a better version of you, you can accomplish any goal, any dream, improve any relationship (personal or business), and create success in all facets of your life. The bottom line is that you will live a more positive, happy, fulfilled, and prosperous life.

Definition of Influence (noun): The capacity to have an effect on the character, development, or behavior of someone or something, or the effect itself.

Synonyms: Affect, impact, determine, sway, guide, shape, change, alter, transform.

Influence (verb): Have an influence.

Synonyms: Effect, impact, sway, authority, guidance, direction.

Here's my personal definition: Persons of influence have personally developed themselves to a point where others follow them voluntarily. They have the ability to change the thoughts, actions, beliefs, and behaviors of others voluntarily.

This book is a guide to influence. Influence allows you the ability to be a leader in your personal life, business life, and with your customers. In your personal life, you will have the respect of friends and family. They will look up to you and allow you to alter their thoughts and beliefs. Influence allows others to place you in a position of authority. When you have influence, others follow you voluntarily. Influence motivates your team to perform better and to go above and beyond without being asked. Influence with your customers helps build your relationships through trust. This trust allows you to be their go-to person. Becoming an individual of influence is hugely important because it improves every facet of your life. When you have the ability to change, alter, impact, shape, and transform the thoughts, actions, beliefs, and behaviors of others, you are a leader who can impact the world around you.

I have read hundreds of books with titles that include the words "leadership" or "leader." The interesting thing to me is that most of these books were mainly about managing, not leading. Most of them never mentioned the importance of becoming a person of influence. Yet, if you aren't a person of influence, you're only a manager or boss. Your team, your customers, and the people in your personal life will do only what they are told to do, no more and probably less. I want to clarify the differences between influential leadership and management.

I have been a student of leaders and leadership for thirty-six years. I have also been a leader to individuals, groups, teams, independent business owners and companies, and have helped them all reach their higher potential and purpose. The book you are about to read is a culmination of my experience and study. If your goal is to have influence and transform yourself into a leader in every facet of your life, then this book is a must read. My purpose is to help individuals gain influence in their personal relationships, sales relationships, and corporate team relationships.

In order to clarify leadership versus management, I will explain the different management styles, which include, but aren't limited to: positional, authoritarian, pace setter, situational, laissez-faire, and transactional. Leadership styles include, without being limited to: paternalistic, charismatic, innovative, servant, transformational, and true influencer.

I will also explain the difference between leadership and management. Finally, and most importantly, this book will explain what true influence is and how you can become a person of influence. By studying this book, you will get a clear vision of true influence and why it is so important to your success in life. Further, you will understand what it takes for you to become a person of influence, so you can maximize your life success.

Many people promoted to positions of authority think they are leaders because of that position. But promotion only makes you the boss, not the leader. As you read on, you will come across some concise statements, centered, in boldface type, that I hope you will remember as my guideposts to what you're about. Here's the first:

> **Leaders have a position of authority, not because of a title, but because of who they are.**

To be a leader, you must have voluntary followers. If you don't have people following you voluntarily, you're just going for a walk.

> **Leadership is a gift from your followers. To earn it, you must become the person others want to follow.**

We will look at the difference between leadership and management. We will consider the goals of true influence and leadership. And, once we have done that, I will ask each of you to answer questions to establish where you are currently as either a manager or leader. You will also have the opportunity to figure out where you want to be along with a plan to get there.

Once you become a true influencer, the lasting benefits to you and your company will be seen by the culture you create: how it impacts results both personally and professionally, how teams react to you as an influencer/leader, how you as an influencer and role model change the world around you and improve the world of others. By becoming a person of influence, you will impact everyone and everything you come into contact with.

By the end of this book, you will know whether you are a leader or merely a manager. You will know what you need to do to move from being a manager to becoming a leader. You will also know what a person with true influence is and how to become such a person. If you decide to become a person of influence, you will live a more positive, productive, happy, and then read on and take action as necessary. I have great confidence that the content in this book will bring you many life benefits.

Questions for thought before you begin:

Do you currently see yourself as a manager or leader?

Do you currently see yourself as a person of influence?

Are you doing the extra personal development work necessary to become a person of influence?

Chapter 1

TYPES OF MANAGEMENT OR LEADERSHIP

Most people who oversee, manage, supervise, or lead others think of themselves as leaders. Over and over in this book, however, I will emphasize the reality that just because you supervise, manage, or oversee people, it doesn't make you a leader. Nor, more importantly, does it make you an influencer. I must emphasize the distinction in order to help you become a true leader.

As you read this chapter on the different varieties of management and leadership, you will come to understand that people who manage or lead others do so using many different management and leadership styles. Look honestly at yourself and what style or styles you are currently using. I will explain the characteristics of the styles, as well as the positives and negatives of the styles.

> **You manage processes, but you lead people.**

My goal with this book is to show you where you are and help you transform into a person of influence, a true leader.

I've drawn the titles of the various management and leadership styles, with information about them, from two sources:

1. "8 Common Leadership Styles," *Association Now*, January 2013, by Rhea Blanken, FASAE.
2. "Leadership Style," WOW.com, source http://en.wikipedia. org/wiki/leadership_style. Updated: 2017-05-25T 16:00Z.

MANAGEMENT STYLES

POSITIONAL

How many of you remember either working for a newly promoted manager, or when you were newly promoted yourself?

I want to share my personal experience and observation about newly promoted managers, having worked for one in my first years in corporate America. Let's call him David, as that was in fact his name. David's management style frustrated me so that I could barely stand working with him or going to his meetings. David didn't know what he was doing or why he was doing it. In those meetings, David took twice as long to explain our monthly goals and the direction we needed to take to achieve them as a manager who'd been on top of his game. David explained things over and over—not because we didn't understand, but because he simply didn't get it. I'm glad I survived David.

I think David was such an inept manager because there is actually very limited training on how to be a leader. The training most managers receive is about process and what's expected—not about how to be a leader. Most of us in corporate life have been promoted because we were good at our previous positions. But that doesn't necessarily make you a good manager, and it certainly doesn't mean you're a leader.

Here is how it happened to me. Those above in the pecking order say, "You've been promoted, and here's your new team." It's like having a new baby without a book about infant care. What happens to most new managers? In most cases, they manage the new team the way they were managed, because that's all they know. I don't know about all of you, but I was scared when I conducted my first team meeting. Most new managers were mentored by managers, not leaders, so they use the power of the position and tell the team what to do, how to do it, when to do it, and to just do. I was blessed, because I'd had others in my life who mentored me on leadership. By the way, David was demoted to an entry-level sales position, because he never grew into a leader.

Normally, when someone is newly promoted, he or she will manage based on the authority of the position. A lot of managers do not develop, however, and continue to manage on that same basis. "I'm the boss," they think, "and they need to do what they're told." This manager doesn't know any other way and doesn't do anything to improve or grow into a leader. This manager remains a manager and will not become a person of influence. When this type of style is used, people are told what to do and when to do it. The people being told what to do and when to do it only do the tasks they are ordered to do. They will do no more than asked and probably less. They respond because they have to, not because they want to. This style of management utilizes power and positional authority to try to get things done through others.

The negative to this is that people being managed in this manner normally are resentful towards the manager. They don't respect the newly promoted manager, because respect is earned over time. The manager's skills have not yet been proven, and relationships have not been established and or progressed to a healthy level.

As a new manager of people, or if you are stuck in this management style, it is very important that you either personally work on yourself or find a mentor to help you grow as a leader and move out of this style. If you remain in this style of management, you will most likely be let go, or else you will move to the next style of management and become an authoritarian, also known as a dictator.

AUTHORITARIAN OR DICTATORIAL

I worked for a guy named Ed for several years. Oh my, was he a dictator. He demanded that things be done, and done his way. He only told you what you did wrong and never said what you did right or well. Everyone working under him was fearful of losing their jobs, and motivation was extremely low. I was blessed at this time, though, because my team had some of the best results in the region. Yet despite my team's results, Ed never acknowledged these successes. His management, his lack of real leadership, was so stifling that I left the company after fifteen years of service to become chief operating officer (COO) with another company.

The authoritarian manager will demotivate, or manage out, great leaders or potentially great leaders. As you read the description below, if this is you, I encourage you to change before you lose your best people. Ed was terminated shortly after he lost several good employees.

Since this management style is usually built on fear, communication is normally only one way between manager and subordinate. The one-way communication of this style is primarily downward. This manager controls discussions and dominates most interactions. The person using this management style gives no room for dialogue or complaining. He or she wants control of what is done, how it is done, when it is done. This manager is also a micromanager, basically giving orders to followers because "I'm the boss and I want everyone to know it."

This management style and resultant work environment have many negative effects. In such a situation it is very difficult to retain the most promising followers or employees. The best people want to be part of the process. They often want to work with and be mentored by someone they look up to and respect. In this scenario, the followers or employees will only do what they are told. They will take no initiative, nor be proactive to move forward. They will wait to be told because they are managed by fear. This management style will only meet its goals but never consistently exceed them. The reason for mediocre results is that followers won't go above and beyond for a manager they don't look up to or respect. This style limits and stifles individual thinking and the followers' growth and ability to become a future leader.

TRANSACTIONAL

Chuck was my transactional manager. Chuck knew every rule and every process like the back of his hand. The only thing that mattered to Chuck was that those he managed followed the rules to the letter and the process from start to finish. Chuck was always managing the process and checking that the rules were being followed. He didn't really care about anything else, including the team. One thing I've learned is that your team doesn't care how much you know until they know how much you care *about them*. Chuck's team had less motivation and inspiration even than the ones mentioned. The team had no freedom and no say on how to do things, even if someone else's idea could produce better results.

Chuck, too, was demoted from a section manager, two levels down to an entry-level manager.

The goal in this management style is to increase productivity and efficiency by improving processes, routines, and procedures. Transactional managers are interested in elevating the followers or workers into a mature team through organization, training, and good habits. They are not, unfortunately, interested in changing or improving the company. They are more interested in following existing rules. The motivation they use to push followers to reach their production goals are rewards for good performance—financial, material, or recognition.

A side note: Recognition is the number-one motivator for followers. The manager who uses this style allows his followers or workers to work independently, only getting involved when production goals are not reached. At this point, the manager retrains the followers on the processes and tasks to improve the production to acceptable levels.

The negative of this style is that, if used exclusively, it will not lead to massive success in a team or organization. This style is minimal on the influence or leadership scale—it is primarily only management. The workers are still being told what to do, when to do it, and how to do it. The full rules are always kept in force. There may be some independence, but a very low tolerance for low performance before the manager gets involved. So, the workers have very little chance to grow and become leaders themselves.

This type of manager has some respect from the workers based on their skill level, but a lack of respect based on character and caring. This keeps the workers as just workers, not followers. This manager does not yet have influence to gain followers from his or her team of workers.

Pace Setter or Driver

A pace-setter manager is often a person who has the same high expectations for others and for him- or herself. Such managers usually have very little patience for those who can't perform up to their level or example. A pace-setter manager (a driver) will often embarrass others for their lack of performance. This manager needs to learn humility and empathy. I've noticed that in sports as well as business, the best player doesn't always make a good coach.

A pace setter was usually the star performer, highly skilled, at his or her previous level, someone who never simply exceeded their goals but crushed them. These people normally bring high expectations of themselves and of others. They do have one leadership quality, namely, they lead by example.

Negatives sometimes occur when the pace setter is promoted to a managerial or leadership role. There can be residual jealousy among their previous peers, and the pace-setter manager usually has very little patience for nonperformers. This manager normally sets very high goals for workers, and raising the bar even higher kills motivation because the workers usually can't even reach the first goals. Although the pace-setter manager was highly skilled in the performance of the previous job, he or she is unable to transfer that knowledge to their workers. They are basically out of touch with the fundamentals and functions of the job process.

This type of manager also operates from a position of high ego: "I did it! Why can't you?" To gain trust and influence, this manager needs to work on his or her own character, beginning with integrity and humility.

LAISSEZ-FAIRE

Marvin was my laissez-faire manager. He was an extremely nice person but lacked the energy or skills to manage, let alone lead. Marvin would let us do whatever we thought we should as long as the job got done. He did not train, guide, or provide feedback to the team. He was a long-term employee and was just holding on until retirement. A lack of passion and leadership is usually a detriment to the team and to the company. Unless some team member steps up to lead, there will be no one prepared, trained, or qualified to take the laissez-faire manager's place. In our group, I stepped up to lead the team (not manage) and was soon promoted, while Marvin, sadly, was fired.

This particular management style is used mainly by individuals with an easygoing personality. Fear or control play no part in this management style, as all power to make decisions is given to the workers. These workers have complete freedom to make decisions about completion of their work. The laissez-faire manager may be aware of what the workers are doing, but rarely gets involved. He or she remains connected to the team only by monitoring performance and production, providing feedback to the workers only on data accumulated through their monitoring. This management style is very—too—trusting and takes other people at their word.

Laissez-faire management's limitations include the following: This style can be used only when workers are self-motivated, skilled at their jobs, highly experienced, and worthy of complete trust. If these circumstances don't exist, this style can never be successful. For this is not leadership or influence, and it's not even management. While the workers like and appreciate the freedom and responsibility, this environment doesn't prepare them to become leaders or influencers in the future. They have no one to look up to. There is no leading by example. The laissez-faire boss isn't respected for his or her skill level, because the workers never perceive what it is. The workers are not mentored, not trained or developed for the next level. They are destined to remain where they are, unless by some means they foster their own development to become persons of influence.

Now that we've discussed several styles of management, look honestly at yourself and decide whether one of these management styles applies to you.

Does one currently fit?

Are you interested in becoming a leader with influence?

Are you willing to change your style and thinking to become a leader?

LEADERSHIP STYLES

Now that we've considered several styles of management, it's time to look at the various styles of leadership. Remember, there's a difference, and it's significant.

> **A leader has authority, not because of title or position, but because of the person he or she has become.**

Someone who moves into one of these leadership styles, as opposed to management styles, that person has earned the respect of followers. He or she has grown personally and become more influential. While these styles do not necessarily represent true

19

influence, someone who has done the personal work to move from a management role to a leadership role now has followers who look up to him or her because of who the leader has become.

As stated earlier, others have given that person a gift in following him or her because *they want to*. Again, they are not required to follow, they choose to follow. The styles we will discuss here include, but are not limited to, the following: paternalistic, situational, charismatic, innovative, servant, democratic, transformational, and true influencer. The more of these styles you use as a leader, the higher level of leadership and influence you will have.

PATERNALISTIC

In paternalistic leadership, the leader acts much like a father or mother figure. This leadership style is one of caring and concern for the followers. Such caring and concern builds loyalty and commitment with followers, who trust this leadership style and normally stay with the company longer because of it. These followers stay the course and don't veer off to work independently. The leader and team act together like a family, both at work and outside of work. They share problems and victories alike. This leadership style also puts in place an award system. As a team, the followers are able to complete more work, because they want to make their leader proud. Paternalistic leadership need not, however, be the only style to achieve long-term success. To have true influence and become a great leader with influence, you must employ many styles and choose the appropriate style at the appropriate time.

Here are some realities to consider regarding paternalistic leadership. This type of leadership carries a possibility of playing favorites within the team. The leader may exclude those followers who seem less loyal. Today, because most companies no longer exhibit deep loyalty toward their employees, this leadership style is not often seen. When followers (employees) don't feel secure in their jobs, loyalty between follower and leader isn't as strong. If, however, the company has fostered a caring culture, the employees (followers) will feel secure with their jobs creating productive results.

Situational

Situational leadership is a coaching style. A great coach can change his style to fit the player or, in this case, the worker. This style of leadership understands the readiness of the group. Based on the individual's needs, the leader will be directive or supportive, at the same time looking for opportunities to be empowering through coaching. Situational leadership creates comfort in the followers, along with a sense of trust and commitment. This is an excellent leadership style to employ when there is a need to reinvent or refine the processes and fundamentals of the followers. This style has many positives and is the beginning stage of influence.

The positive aspect of situational leadership is that when the leader connects appropriate behavior to individual followers' needs, workers' comfort level rises and uncertainty within the group diminishes. This style of leadership also improves work and brings out and calls on individual followers' strengths. The negative aspects of situational leadership are few. The first negative is that if followers behave unpredictably or change unexpectedly, it can be confusing to the group and damage or lower production. Second, if the leader lacks the ability to read individuals' needs correctly, this style will not work.

CHARISMATIC

Individuals who can use this style of leadership have charismatic personalities. They are able to use the power of their charisma to attract and influence others with their magnetic personality. They are able to motivate their followers to move forward through their energy and self-confidence in their cause, goals, vision, or mission. This leader is very positive and attracts followers based on that positivity. Followers voluntarily follow such a leader, especially when they, too, believe in the leader's cause, goals, vision, or mission. The passion this leadership style brings with it is also inspiring to followers. A charismatic leader is seen as very likable by his or her followers. Oprah Winfrey is an excellent example of such a leader.

The positives of this type of leadership are many. This leader has taken a big step toward influence with his or her followers, though not yet at the highest level. Charismatic leaders have the ability to inspire others to action. This leadership style is also great at raising followers' morale, keeping them inspired and motivated at a higher level. By inspiring action and improving morale, such a leader's followers or teams are well positioned to reach higher levels of success or increase the organization's market reach. Another positive aspect of charismatic leaders is their ability to bring previous employees along with them. In addition, charismatic leaders are natural recruiters.

Even though there are many positives to this style of leadership, there are also some negatives. One negative is that, because this type of leadership is based totally on the leader's charisma and personality, if the leader leaves the group or organization, the followers or team will feel lost and flounder, and their individual productivity and that of the group will decline. A second negative for this leadership style is often that the leader believes more in him- or herself than in the followers. In addition, the charismatic leader may be so confident that he or she will take on more risk than the group can handle.

Fred "Chip" Kron (pictured), currently executive vice president of Amerifirst Financial, and former vice president and owner, Great Southwest Mortgage, is an outstanding example of a leader who is both charismatic and paternalistic.

I have known Fred Kron since June 2001, which makes this a fifteen-year relationship. In 1995, Fred and his partner Eric Lutz co-founded a mortgage company they called Great Southwest Mortgage, with Fred as vice president. Fred and Eric grew this company from one office in 1995 to 100 offices in three states by 2008. In fact, Great Southwest Mortgage was the largest mortgage lender in Arizona, surpassing such companies as Wells Fargo. After Great Southwest Mortgage discontinued business because of the market crash of 2008, Fred was hired as executive vice president of Amerifirst Financial, continuing the same level of success with Amerifirst Financial that he enjoyed at Great Southwest Mortgage.

Fred is a leader whom I respect and admire. When I was looking for a new job opportunity, my wife Donna wanted me to interview with two mortgage companies, one being Great Southwest Mortgage with Eric Lutz and Fred Kron at the helm. The other company was owned and operated by Dave Heuermann, another leader whom I interviewed for this book. She and I felt strongly about the integrity and leadership of both companies and their leadership teams. As you know by now, the quality I expect most in a leader is integrity.

Without integrity, the leader won't have or gain trust or, more importantly, influence. Fred Kron is a leader who has the character qualities to be a great leader and influencer.

As Fred and I began our discussion about this book, the first item I wanted to discuss was his view of management versus leadership. Fred's take on the topic was unique. He said, "A manager is someone you're assigned to. A leader is someone you pick." I thought this was an excellent distinction, for it goes along with a personal belief of mine: Leadership is a gift from your followers. To earn it, you must become the person others want to follow.

Fred went on to say, "A leader is all the things he asks others to be and is willing to do what he asks them to do." Leading by example is a quality at the top of his leadership list. As Fred expanded his reflections on leadership, he talked about the mental philosophy he felt was important. "People in leadership work *with* people," he said, "as opposed to having people working *for* them." To me, that simple statement makes a good philosophical distinction between the perspective of a manager versus that of a leader.

As Fred and I talked about qualities that make a great leader, one of the first qualities he mentioned was integrity. "Without integrity," he stated confidently, "you cannot gain trust with your followers. Without trust and honesty, you won't have respect and influence with your team." Another quality that Fred emphasized was the importance of caring for your people. Fred told me he takes time to really get to know his team, listen to them with sincere interest, and be genuine with them. He feels strongly that this helps him to be in tune with his team.

In this same vein, Fred spoke about being caring and empathic toward your team, and how going the extra mile for them is very important as well. Humility is a quality that Fred spoke of at great length. He stated that humility was a quality he had gained through business and personal adversities later in his career. Based on those adversities, Fred gained humility and realized just how important this quality is for a leader. In fact, he went on to say that he had previously thought of it as a weakness. Now, Fred sees humility as a big strength in his character as a leader. It shows his people that he's human, not perfect, does make mistakes. His humility makes him more approachable and his leadership team more comfortable around him.

People skills is another quality Fred sees as very important, including a leader's emotional intelligence. This enables a leader to be effective and to lead different personality types. Without people skills, it is impossible to lead people. In summary, Fred stated, leaders must never forget the importance of people skills, remember to demonstrate humility when dealing with people and challenges, always keep a clear vision for the team to follow, and stay flexible and open to change when and where needed to accomplish the leader's vision.

The last thing Fred and I discussed was a leader's responsibility to develop and help the team grow. He believes developing more leaders is the lifeblood of a company and provides its ability to grow. During this discussion, Fred brought up yet another great point, namely, that most companies, including his current company, have no formal plan to develop leaders or the qualities and character needed for great leadership. Fred is correct. It is a big problem for companies, but there is a solution through personal development. Seeing this need for personal development, I started my own business to help companies and individuals reach higher levels and goals: #ElevateYourGame.

INNOVATIVE

An innovative style of leadership calls for its practitioners to look at and do things outside the normal box. They are visionaries and set very high goals. In this style of leadership, leaders hold the greatest vision of what could be. They will then go above and beyond the normal course of action. Since this style of leadership is so forward thinking, when things aren't working according to plan these leaders bring in new ideas and change course when necessary.

An example of this style of leadership is Richard Branson. When asked by *Inc.* magazine to share his philosophy, he said, "Dream big by setting yourself seemingly impossible challenges. You then have to catch up to them."

This style of leadership has many positives for both the followers and the organization. Innovative leadership allows for more freedom and risk taking throughout the organization. It also creates a safe environment for free-flowing ideas and an atmosphere of respect for all ideas and individuals. When there are failures, it doesn't slow down the progress of ideas, just the change of direction. Followers in this environment have a far higher level of job satisfaction. They also have an elevated level of commitment and respect for the leader. With a higher level of job satisfaction, they remain with the leader or organization for longer periods of time. And if this leadership style is coupled with personal development to achieve a higher level of influence, it will be extremely effective.

The innovative style of leadership carries very few negatives or cautions. One negative could, however, arise if the risks are too outrageous, with things getting out of hand, wasting time and costs on ineffective ideas. Beyond that, followers need an excellent understanding of the end vision or goal, for they will then create effective ideas.

One person I interviewed who uses this leadership style, as well as being a servant leader, is Russell Williamson (pictured).

I was quite excited and interested in discussing leadership perspectives with Russell. Now a performance consultant/project manager at Ascend LLC, Russell is a former staff sergeant, Special Operations Air Force Warfare Center. I wanted to hear this 28-year-old millennial's thoughts on effective leadership and his perspective on leading other millennials.

Our discussion revealed that Russell had a sound foundation for leadership qualities. I've known Russell for seventeen years and have seen him mature in both age and life perspectives. He has always been a sharp, intuitive, and creative young man, shaped for leadership by various life factors. One of these factors was his upbringing. Russell's parents, his father Russell, Sr., and his mother, Debbie Williamson, raised young Russell with a strong moral background. Qualities he has always displayed include integrity, honesty, responsibility, courage, and leading by example.

Russell was never a youngster who needed to follow the crowd. In high school he never folded to peer pressure in his morality, values, or personal qualities. His strength of character earned him a lot of respect and admiration from his peers. He has been leading by example from his teen years. Beyond that, eight years of military service as a special operations advisor added discipline to his leadership skill set. Military service also increased his creative and innovative problem-solving skills. As a staff sergeant, he learned to motivate, inspire, and lead a group of men. Russell spent one year with the United States Air Force as a program manager in the Special Operations Air Warfare Center, and for the last year he has worked for Ascend LLC as a performance consultant/project manager. In this capacity he trains workers on oil rigs about leadership and optimizing performance. Russell pointed out to me that these workers are tough, rough-and-tumble manly men in physically demanding and dangerous jobs. In working with them, initially his greatest challenge was his youth, as many of the men are much older and have far more experience in that environment than Russell.

Even so, by his innovative approach, he was able to gain the respect of these older, more experienced men. Beyond that, Russell maintains humility, starting his leadership training by stating that he knows they have more experience than he. He goes on to tell them that he wants them to share their ideas with him. In that way, he gets the men engaged so that Russell can also share some of his ideas with them. This exchange breaks down barriers and walls and builds mutual respect between Russell and his teams on the rig.

Here is how Russell views the difference between leadership and management: "A manager is someone who gives out tasks to be done, while a leader inspires and motivates his followers to accomplish their tasks." Russell told me that he believes a good leader must know himself or herself well and truly know the people being led. To get to know your followers, Russell said, takes caring about your people and genuinely listening to them. He also stated that a good leader needs a clear vision and good communication skills to be able to share that vision with others. "Good leaders need to know their own faults," he told me, "so they can empower their people to help in those areas."

The ability to inspire and motivate one's team is also a feature of Russell's list of leadership qualities.

In his view, the qualities a great leader needs in order to have influence include integrity, honesty, trust, humility, self-awareness, courage, listening skills, responsibility, and the ability to inspire and motivate. I found this list interesting because it listed the same qualities I had heard from other leaders I interviewed. While half the age of many experienced leaders, Russell already has a fund of knowledge equal to that of leaders with far more years of experience and personal growth.

I asked Russell, as both a millennial and a leader, what he sees as the biggest motivating factor for his peers. "Recognition," he said. "Recognition is the best motivator." In my own thirty-five years of leadership experience, I have found the same thing. Throughout my career, recognition has always been the number-one motivator. Many people think of a raise or a bonus as being more effective, but I've found more money to be a short-term motivator. Once the bonus is spent or the raise has been absorbed into your budget, it's forgotten. But when you give someone recognition, it earns them more respect from their peers, boosts their confidence, and improves their production over the long term. In that knowledge, too, Russell is way beyond his years and very intuitive in his leadership views.

Russell told me a great story that fits right in with the philosophy of this book. He was conducting a leadership training aboard an oil rig with about seventy participants. In the training, Russell was explaining that it was possible for anyone to become a leader. During one of the breaks, when he was on an elevator with one of the senior managers, this person told him he didn't agree with that statement. He went on to say that there was a guy on the rig they called Kat who could never be a leader, because Kat just didn't have what it took.

After the break the training continued. At the end of the day, Russell asked the group to look at some words they put on the board about leadership, then come back the next day and discuss their thoughts and experience with one of those words as a group.

When the time came, Russell asked for volunteers, but no one came forward. After a few minutes when the silence started to be a little awkward, Kat volunteered to speak about some of the words. And as Kat spoke, he did it with confidence and articulated very well. Once Kat was done, the rest of the group took up the discussion. After the training ended, the person who'd said Kat couldn't be a leader admitted he was wrong. As a result of Kat's participation that day, Kat gained respect from that manager and his peers, along with more self-confidence.

To add to the above, Kat used assertiveness—one of the best qualities of a leader. Many others considered themselves leaders, yet they didn't step up to lead and participate in the discussion. It was Kat who stepped forward to break the awkward silence, thus influencing others to follow him.

SERVANT

A servant leader is focused on the success of others first. With this style of leadership, the followers, the organization, and the leader all prosper. Servant leadership is built on high standards of character. A leader's character is the most important ingredient to create true influence. Servant leadership carries many of the character traits needed for true influence. The first of these character traits is honor. The servant leader honors others above him- or herself. Some other qualities inherent in this style are open-mindedness and excellent listening skills.

A servant leader will celebrate the success of the individuals and the teams. Second, servant leaders value ethics and integrity above profit. To accomplish this, they must be above board in all their dealings, even behind closed doors. The promise or word given by servant leaders is their bond. Third, a servant leader aims to empower others without concern for personal gain, sharing credit and responsibility for success and failures. Such leaders look at failures as an opportunity and a learning experience to move forward. Fourth, servant leaders have a strong vision and inspire others to engage in that vision. The qualities here are modeling their inner passion, belief, and commitment to that vision and those goals. They also have excellent communication skills and articulate the vision, goals, and plans to their followers. Fifth, servant leaders keep a balance between their focus on goals and vision yet stay flexible when it's necessary to go in a different direction. The servant leader's mindset here is valuing long-term gains over short-term success. Sixth, a servant leader has great self-confidence, yet leads through humility—a great strength. Followers are considered more important than the leader. Humility also allows servant leaders to openly take responsibility for their mistakes. Seventh, a servant leader puts the followers' interests before tasks. This is accomplished by being kind and caring when the pressure rises. The servant leader also recognizes, acknowledges, and shows appreciation to the followers. In order to get to this level of leadership, the servant leader has done a lot of personal development. The servant leader also has a high level of influence. To get to the highest level of influence, the servant leader should continue this personal development, retain a mentor, and remain teachable. A great example of this type of leader would be Herb Kelleher former CEO of Southwest Airlines.

The positive aspects of this style of leadership are many. The followers have a high level of commitment to their leader and the organization. They also have a high level of job satisfaction. When interviewed, the followers will express some of the following attitudes: Love for their job, love for their leader, willing to go above and beyond without being asked, follow their leader because they want to, not because they are required to.

Servant leadership carries few negatives. The chief one I see is when control over followers is needed. The servant leader will have difficulty reclaiming that control from the followers she or he has empowered. It is also difficult for the servant leader to let people go who aren't performing.

Pictured here is an interview with someone who is a servant leader, as well as a charismatic and paternalistic one. For fifteen years I have known Dave Heuermann and always had the highest respect for him. I was thrilled that he agreed to be interviewed about his perspective on leadership.

Dave founded his own mortgage company, Axis Mortgage, serving as owner and president in the greater Phoenix area from 1999 to 2006. Later, from 2007 to 2015, he was chief production officer for Wallick & Volk Mortgage Bankers and is currently vice president for the Mountain West Region of HomeStreet Bank. It's clear that Dave has extensive experience running companies and leading people.

When I asked Dave his view of leadership versus management, he told me he sees management as a form of control. "You manage things," he said, "and you manage processes, but you lead people." Dave went on to enumerate the qualities of a great leader. First, he believes a leader must lead by example, from the front. A great leader must also have integrity, which he sees as one of the foundations of leadership. Then, too, a leader must have excellent listening skills at several levels. Here Dave went into detail: listening to understand the needs of the individuals, listening to understand the full message of what the individual is delivering, and listening in order to learn and grow. In his view, listening skills are a hugely important way to let followers know you understand and care about them. Strong listening skills add value to the followers, builds their self-confidence, and inspires them to work harder.

In Dave's opinion, another important skill for great leadership is willingness to make decisions. He summed up his leadership philosophy this way: lead from the front so you can put people in positions where they are happy, put yourself in your followers' shoes so you can be empathic, listen to your followers for understanding, and continue learning and growing as a leader. Dave's goal is to help others reach their success first, thus creating his own success. Above all, Dave strives to be genuine, caring, honest, and a person of integrity. For without honesty there can be no trust, and without a foundation of trust, building relationships or success for a company will be impossible.

TRANSFORMATIONAL

The transformational style of leadership requires some of the same skills and traits essential for charismatic leadership. The transformational leader's goal is to transform or change the thinking of the followers. Transformational leadership requires very high levels of communication to get followers to attain their goals and change their thinking. This type of leader is highly visible in the work environment, has the big picture, and clearly communicates that vision and those goals to the company or group. This type of leader focuses on major things and delegates lesser tasks to followers. This leadership style inspires its followers by gaining their buy-in to the vision or goal and gives the followers a sense of purpose.

Transformational leadership has several positive aspects. The transformational leader leads by example and is involved in the process with the followers. This style can lead to a high level of productivity for all team members, with followers well engaged in the process.

At the same time, this style of leadership carries some negative aspects. Transformational leadership aims to transform followers' thinking, even if doing so is unwanted or uncomfortable. Followers are expected to give their best at all times, which is difficult without their total commitment. In order for this style to work, the people need to be very detail oriented and organized.

An example of a transformational and servant leader is Tony Lucky Winston (pictured), whom I've known since 1973–our sophomore year in high school, when we played football together. Tony moved after that year, and I lost track of him until four or five years ago. Tony has had many successes in life. One major success is his current business, Digital Media, which he founded. Tony says this business is his passion. He and I both believe that when you find your passion in life, nothing can stop your success. Digital Media, Tony's company, is contracted to Microsoft and creates Windows mobile-phone applications. Tony told me, humbly, that they have more than 350 million customers. This is just a few customers, Tony! I'm so proud of you!

As Tony and I talked, the first thing I wanted to know was his view of leadership versus management. Tony's answer was short and to the point. He said that a manager is more of an administrator. Managers follow rules, policies, and procedures. They don't usually allow thinking outside the box from their people. A leader, on the other hand, is always looking for ways to improve the process, ideas, people, production, and the company.

The next item Tony and I discussed was what qualities he believes make a great leader. The first thing out of Tony's mouth? "A teller of the truth"—in other words, integrity. Honesty was the second quality Tony mentioned. Without integrity and honesty there can be no trust from your followers. Without trust, you cannot build respect and relationships. Without mutual respect and trusting relationships, ideas will not flow freely, stifling the company and its growth. As another important quality, Tony also talked about effective communication. Effective communication allows the leader to share the vision, direction, and plan with the rest of the team. Clear, effective communication puts everyone on the same page when the company needs to change direction and move forward.

One of the last qualities Tony touched on was the importance of a positive attitude, which he calls "a winning spirit." Tony feels that a positive attitude is hugely important, because your attitude creates a self-fulfilling prophecy. Your mind is a powerful tool to create your reality. Tony gave a simple sports example. If the coach says, "We probably won't win today," guess what, you won't win that day! Your mind will not create a strategy to win because it has already been shut down by the thought that you won't win today.

Tony also wanted me to know that he believes fully in being a servant leader. He never asks his followers to do anything that he's not willing to do first. That is a great quality and a great leadership style to have.

In a culture based on integrity, honesty, and mutual respect, ideas flow freely. In such an environment, the team is willing to take risks and even to fail. Tony feels this is of utmost importance, because without failure, there can be no success. He and I agree that we've learned more from our failures in life than from our successes. As Tony learned from his failures, he has kept moving forward to his successes.

In addition, Tony stated that his spiritual depth and beliefs have helped him become who he is today as a person and a leader. Later in this book, I will discuss the importance of living a life of excellence, how important spirituality is to a leader.

As Tony and I concluded our conversation about leadership, he told me, "Without character, you cannot be a leader. True character and servant leadership give you influence with those around you." These qualities grant you the gift of leadership.

TRUE INFLUENCE

The top leadership style is the one carrying maximum influence. Every leadership style I've discussed has included some level of influence. Some of the greatest leaders in history have employed many of the styles I've discussed and are able to use the appropriate style for the particular time. A leader may need to be a charismatic, servant, innovative, transformational, paternalistic, or situational leader, depending on the situation.

Every follower responds differently to the various styles I've discussed. Many top leaders are agile in their ability to employ multiple styles to impact and influence different groups of followers. Through this agility, the leader may gain more influence and more followers for several reasons. Such leaders can relate to and inspire more followers, as well as gaining stronger commitment from followers who will go above and beyond. A leader adept at practicing a variety of styles will have more influence, which transfers to higher morale and higher levels of commitment and production. These leaders create a culture followers want to stay with over the long haul.

An outstanding example of such a leader is Jody Weis (pictured). Jody is able to exercise his remarkable gifts at times as servant leader, innovative leader, transactional leader, or situational leader, drawing on all styles.

In the twenty-one years I've known Jody Weis (pictured) and his wife Janice, they've been a couple I've always looked up to and admired. For many years Janice was with the United States Secret Service, charged with protecting the president of the United States. Jody served for five and a half years in the United States Army, for nearly four of those years in command positions with two different units. Leaving the Army with the rank of captain, Jody then joined the Federal Bureau of Investigation to serve for twenty-three years. With the FBI Jody held a range of positions from special agent to deputy assistant director, retiring as special agent in charge, essentially CEO, of the Philadelphia field office. He then accepted an appointment from Chicago's Mayor Richard M. Daley as superintendent of the Chicago Police Department, filling this position for three years, with more than 13,000 officers serving

under him. For nearly thirty years, then, Jody has been in high-level leadership roles

In my interview with Jody about his thoughts on leadership, the first thing he and I discussed was management versus leadership. Jody stated, "Leadership is crafting the vision and selling that vision to your followers. Management is about the process of prioritizing and supplying the necessary resources to support and accomplish the leader's vision."

As we discussed the qualities Jody feels are necessary for great leadership, a list of some of those qualities evolved. First and foremost, Jody grouped together integrity, honesty, and trustworthiness, going on to say that without integrity and honesty, there is no trust. "Without trust," he told me, "you can't have influence with your followers, and without influence, there's no opportunity for leadership. You can manage, because you're in a position of authority, and your followers do what you say because they have to. But for a leader with influence followers do things willingly—because they want to. This is the huge difference in motivation and desire leadership creates among the followers."

The second quality Jody emphasized was leading by example. Jody believes a leader will lead from the front. In order to lead, he told me, you need to be willing to do whatever you are asking others to do. When you are in the mix with your team, he believes, they have a higher level of respect for you as a leader. This in turn gives you a higher level of influence.

The importance of communication skills was another topic Jody stressed. The importance of being able to communicate and sell the vision of the organization to your leadership team, and then to the followers, is something he sees as all-important. If your team and followers lack a clear vision of what is expected and the direction in which they are meant to be going, they most likely will not achieve the desired outcomes or accomplish the mission.

Compassion was the next quality Jody brought up, stating that he sees compassion as critical in leadership. "Followers will make mistakes," he said, "but when a follower makes a mistake, the leader won't throw them away because of the mistake! Instead, an effective leader will use the mistake as a teaching point." In his view, very few actions are lethal for an employee, if the leader deals with the issue swiftly, fairly, with consistency, and moves on. Human resources are the most precious asset in any organization. "When the circumstances allow for compassion," he says, "offer it! This can go far in gaining the followers' trust and confidence."

Hence through compassion, fairness, integrity, and leading by example, a leader will create an environment of trust and collaboration. Where the fear of failure is not a concern, this safe culture will then unlock the team's potential. Otherwise your leadership team and followers wouldn't be willing to take the risk of sharing their ideas. As Jody likes to say, "Take a risk, but don't be reckless. If you fail, fail fast and move on to the next opportunity."

Still more qualities we discussed were commitment and flexibility. Jody stated that a leader needs to be committed to the vision, company, and people he or she leads. He went on to say that along with being committed, a leader also needs to be flexible. Flexibility is so important because we work and live in an ever-changing environment, and in Jody's view a leader must be able to change direction when necessary, to call an audible if you will, to keep the team moving ahead without getting bogged down trying to make a failed plan succeed.

As Jody and I continued our conversation about effective leadership, he stressed building an atmosphere where opinions and ideas are freely expressed. This responsibility falls on the leader, for only she or he can make this work. To quote Jody, "Set up an environment where a rough-and-tumble discussion is allowed to get to a decision, where all opinions, even dissenting ones, are taken into consideration." This environment should make the team totally comfortable in giving and sharing ideas. "An effective leader should also have a philosophy of serving the people being led—in other words, I'm here for you." Jody believes that to be effective you must always support the people you lead.

The last topic Jody and I touched on was the importance of being a leader with influence. "No matter what your title may be," Jody believes, "when you have influence with others, you're a de facto leader." This is someone, he told me, who should be groomed for advancement. Great leaders don't fear being replaced by their followers. In fact, Jody views it as good leadership to hire people who can advance to your level or beyond. It is a leader's responsibility to look for and groom others to be his replacement, for this is how a company replenishes its leadership team and continues to progress. My own opinion, which I state in this book, is that failing to groom other leaders stifles a company's growth and potential for progress.

My discussion with Jody convinced me he commands several styles of leadership. Again, a leader who has the ability to use multiple styles also has a higher level of influence, an ability to relate to different personality types and attain a higher level of leadership. In the case of Jody Weis, the high level of leadership and responsibility he has carried throughout his career makes this obvious.

Another outstanding leader is Lori Tyler (pictured), whom I've known for about ten years. A high achiever at every level of business, she has always been an example of high integrity, honesty, focus, caring, and many other qualities of leadership and character. I'd classify her style above all as situational, in that according to the situation, she can be paternalistic, a servant leader, and a transactional leader. Having spent sixteen years with Lexus Nexus, rising to the position of vice president of marketing, Lori is now vice president of global marketing with AccessData.

During our interview Lori offered an excellent perspective on the challenges a woman faces as she attains a high level of leadership responsibility. What she had to say convinced me that great leadership is the same with both men and women, a high level of character being key. I learned through my discussion with Lori that she went through a lot of self-reflection and personal changes when she was first promoted. She wanted to make sure she looked like a leader, acted like a leader, and communicated like a leader. It was obvious that she was already acting and performing like a leader, or she wouldn't have been promoted. Yet Lori wanted to raise her game to an even higher level. One of her challenges, she explained, was her desire to prove herself.

When asked whether her gender made her believe she might need to do more, to be more businesslike, Lori acknowledged that she felt significant self-induced pressure to act and perform better than her male counterparts. She continues to prove her worth today at this high level of leadership. I point out throughout this book that

41

true influence is when others follow you voluntarily. When Lori left Lexus Nexus, many of her followers there wanted to work for her at AccessData. They followed her voluntarily because of her character and leadership.

One of my early questions for Lori touched on management versus leadership. "I believe in a balanced approach," she said, "between management and leadership." She explained her view that a balance must be maintained between the mechanics or processes and ensuring that your followers have the resources to attain the vision. "Leadership," she continued, "is the people side of the business." She stated the importance for the leader to have a clear vision and communicate that vision in a way that inspires the team. Lori also pointed out the importance of attainable goals and clear expectations. "Individual team members need to know their roles," she said, "the importance of those roles and how their roles contribute to the overall vision."

When I asked Lori what qualities she believes are important for great leadership, she placed primary emphasis on integrity, honesty, mutual respect, and trust. She said that in order to create a culture where everyone feels valued for their contributions and comfortable and free to express ideas, those first four qualities are imperative. "It's been my experience," she stated, "that for a leader with true influence, followers will work harder, do more, and do things willingly—in other words, because they want to." She believes it takes an influential leader to bring about this huge difference in motivation, inspiration, and desire on the part of the followers.

As for other important qualities in leadership, Lori listed being empowering, inspiring, authentic, collaborative, ethical, a good communicator, and having emotional intelligence—all qualities that Lori possesses herself and continues to work on and improve. Lori went into detail on some of these qualities and their application. Empowering individual team members to accomplish their goals, hold the vision, and meet expectations is very important. Enabling team members to take on responsibility and make decisions allows them to grow individually and as a team. They feel more invested in the process and take ownership of the goals and vision. As for communication skills, both spoken and written, Lori feels strongly about the importance of that ability. Good communication skills help to crystallize and deliver the vision, goals, and expectations. As for emotional intelligence, Lori sees that as an element of the people skills imperative for leading others. Lori gave an example of a high-level executive she worked under who knew everything about the mechanics side of the business but lacked the vital people skills that would have made it possible for him to lead, inspire, and influence the employees he was supposed to lead.

On the matter of coaching and constructive criticism, Lori had some excellent insights. She believes that, for any leader, it's important to recognize you aren't always right. It's also important to trust your team and let them run with ideas and direction. To accomplish this, Lori has established an atmosphere where there are no failures, only learning experiences. Doing so gives her an opportunity to mentor and coach her team members, which improves the team and supports ideas moving forward. One last point Lori and I were agreed on—the matter of hiring. Lori believes that to improve the team and the company long term, you must hire people who are better than you.

I pointed out the likelihood that some managers, fearful of losing their jobs, might feel too threatened to hire highly qualified employees. In Lori's experience and mine, however, just the opposite occurs. A leader with highly qualified team members will look better to the company because of the total team performance. Many times this can lead to upward mobility for both the leader and the team members, so that the overall company improves.

My discussion with Lori convinced me that she uses several leadership styles at different times: paternalistic, servant, situational, and transactional. Lori has true influence with her followers, because she is able to lead different types of people with the appropriate style. Such a gifted leader will be able to reach an even higher level of leadership, as Lori herself has done. The evidence was clear when her followers at Lexus Nexus chose to go with her voluntarily to AccessData, where she is currently employed.

Now, look at yourself honestly to determine if you fit one or more of the above leadership styles.

Based on the above leadership styles, which one currently fits you?

Are you interested in becoming a true and ultimate influencer?

Are you willing to continue your personal development and improve your character to the point of having ultimate influence?

Chapter 2

DIFFERENCES BETWEEN LEADERSHIP AND MANAGEMENT

I n the previous chapter, I shared my perspective on management and leadership styles with details about various ones. This chapter will deal with the differences between management and leadership as well as the benefits of leadership over management. Most of you at this point are probably thinking, "What is Gary talking about?" Remember, a position of authority does not automatically make you a leader. Being a leader is not about a title, years of experience, age, or gender.

There are very distinct differences in the mindset of a leader as opposed to that of a manager. There are also big differences in how they oversee and handle the people they work with. A leader will have great influence over the workers, while a manager may have very little. This difference in influence affects commitment level, work ethic, production level, willingness to go above and beyond, and motivation for following. Workers follow leaders because they want to, not because they have to, while the converse is true of managers.

If you believe you're a leader just because you've been promoted, you're living under a huge misconception, and your employees or subordinates probably know it. Promotion to a higher level in a company with others assigned to work under your authority makes you their boss, not necessarily their leader. This is also true when you hire someone new into the company. What do I mean by this statement? Those over whom you have authority will do what you tell them to do because they have to. As previously mentioned, they will usually do only what is asked of them, no more, sometimes less. If you're a manager, your subordinates often do enough to avoid being fired.

In this situation, you have not earned influence; you have only gained authority. In the last chapter, I called this positional management. At this point, most people have not developed themselves personally to become a person of influence or a true leader. I always remind people that you manage processes, but you lead people. My goal in writing this book is to help you move from being a manager to being a leader and influencer, and beyond that to move from utilizing one style to multiple styles of leadership and to teach others so we are encouraging others to grow into leadership roles.

LEADERSHIP VS. MANAGEMENT

I have been blessed to speak to groups all over the country about leadership. Every time I do so, I ask the group for one word that describes a person they look up to and admire, someone who has influenced them or affected their lives in positive ways. Every group comes up with almost the same ten or fifteen words. Here are the most common ones:

1. Integrity
2. Honesty
3. Trustworthy
4. Empowering
5. Fairness
6. Passionate
7. Positive attitude
8. Courageous
9. Caring
10. Great listening skills
11. Great spoken and written communication skills
12. Vision
13. Decisiveness
14. Skilled and knowledgeable at their job
15. Respect their team members

When you add or develop these qualities in yourself, you not only become a leader, you gain influence. Do you notice that about seventy percent of the words are character traits? I don't want to be misleading about the need for skills. I believe leaders need to be knowledgeable about and skilled at their jobs. I also believe that in order to be a true leader, one must become the person others WANT to follow. When that occurs, it indicates a person of influence. Followers will follow this individual voluntarily. In contrast, a skilled manager is someone whose direction subordinates follow because they have to. Most of the time they follow and work out of fear, not because they choose to or want to.

One of the major differences between a manager and a leader is how the followers are used, managed, or led. I have always believed that you manage processes and you lead people. A manager usually functions as a dictator, authoritarian, or with control. Either you do the job the manager's way, or you hit the highway of unemployment.

47

In many cases, a manager operates by instilling fear. Intimidation can also be a tool to motivate followers to do their jobs. Often the manager will look for what the follower is doing wrong without commending the follower for what was done right. The processes that need to be managed could be training on products, the sales process, production numbers, or employee handbook rules and regulations, to name a few. Once the employee or follower is trained, that's the time to lead them to success.

I want to point out how the use of leadership differs from managing. A leader will train on the same processes that require training as the manager does. The real difference occurs once training is completed and the follower is ready to begin working the job or career he or she was hired for. A leader empowers the employee to go out and do the job. A leader will lead from the front and lead by example. Leaders make themselves available for questions, guidance, or additional training when needed to keep the follower on track and moving toward success. A leader will encourage new ideas and ways to get the job or tasks completed. A leader will also look for and give recognition for successes. Leaders will encourage a system of learning to overcome and move forward from mistakes or failures.

The comparison that follows shows the distinct differences between a leadership mindset and a managerial mindset. The source of this information is Stephen Covey, Philip Morris USA training course 1983.

Leadership vs. Manager Mindset

Leaders shape the actions taken – Managers chase the input
Leaders focus on group success – Managers focus on individual jobs
Leaders encourage new ideas.
Managers enforce the old ones.
Leaders stimulate right things.
Managers monitor wrong things.
Leaders thrive through competition
Managers talk little of competition.
Leaders prize comparison with others.
Managers see scant need for comparison.
Leaders think of involvement programs.
Managers think of suggestion programs.
Leaders empower others to make decisions.
Managers tightly control the decision process.
Leaders see leading as animate and proactive.
Managers see managing as inanimate and reactive.
Leaders think of dynamic, caring, and human systems.
Managers think of a business following a script.
Leaders think of improving initiative and innovation.
Managers think of improving compliance and conformance.
Leaders shape organization character, culture, and climate.
Managers assume that's neither a big deal – nor their Job.
Leaders provide vision; Managers carry it out.
Leaders make it better; Managers make it run.
Leaders make it happen; Managers hope it happens.
Leaders gain business; Managers maintain business.
Leaders create more leaders. Managers create more managers.

POLICIES, RULES, AND PRINCIPLES

In all businesses there are policies, procedures, and rules. Each of us has our own moral compass and the principles we live by as individuals and as leaders. One thing for certain is that the policies, procedures, and rules of a company can and sometimes do change. As managers come and go in a company, all of them will have their own sets of rules by which they manage. These management rules will be based on whatever style of management that they use. These rules or policies may also change when a company is going through a business downturn. Stress and pressure can create big changes in the rules and how business is done, with pressure exerted on the followers and the fear factor used to push performance to a higher level. As a manager, you have no choice but to use more pressure, fear, and intimidation on the followers. The followers will not voluntarily work harder for a manager who hasn't developed himself into a leader with influence. The manager has no other choice but negative pressure to get the job done.

As a leader, however, your moral compass and principles will remain constant. A leader will follow the policies, procedures, and rules of the company but remain flexible for changes that may occur in these areas. If the leader continues to develop and improve him- or herself, character, integrity, and influence will develop as well, and principles will grow to higher levels. Leaders are focused yet flexible. When their followers emulate this same mindset and principles, they, too will reach higher levels of success without as much pressure when rule changes occur. With this flexibility, there is usually no slowdown in production, though if there is a slowdown, it is very short lived. The reason for this is that followers will work harder, put in extra time when necessary, and do more than they're required to do because of their respect for the leader and his or her influence.

The comparisons in this chapter of the differences between a manager and a leader are huge. Someone who grows into a leader instead of remaining a manager creates a massive difference in every area of business and personal relationships. Leadership and true influence improve morale, production, teamwork, commitment level, follower longevity with the company, job satisfaction, new ideas, higher performance, and better relationships.

What style of management do you currently use?

If you are still a manager, what style of leadership do you want to develop?

When will you make the decision to begin your conversion to leadership?

What areas do you need to improve or change to become a person of influence?

What type of leadership style do you currently use?

What style of leadership can you add to improve as a leader?

Chapter 3

THE GOAL IS LEADERSHIP

> **By becoming a person of influence,**
> **you become a leader.**

The previous chapter ended with enumeration of some of the benefits that follow when a manager becomes a leader. Continuing this discussion, because leadership can produce almost unlimited improvements beyond mere management, the focus here will be confined to key areas.

First, the use of management styles will stifle the growth of a company or business. Using management styles only maintains the status quo. The manager normally doesn't prepare followers for his replacement. This stifling usually occurs because the manager is afraid of being replaced and not qualified to move up.

The leadership view, on the other hand, is about improvement of the team. The goal then is to intentionally develop followers into leaders who can replace the current leader. John F. Kennedy stated the view of the leader best: "The rising tide lifts all boats." The bottom line here is that managers create more managers, while leaders create more leaders, leading to growth and expansion for the business.

Second, leaders focus on group success. Managers focus on individual jobs and what's going wrong. This negativity is another example of stifling business growth. In this example, a manager is monitoring each job, making sure the followers are doing their jobs correctly. The leader, conversely, is looking at the whole group's performance and success in relation to goals and vision. Leadership is more proactive, creating a visionary perspective. When everyone performs better, goals are surpassed and the vision is realized.

Third, leaders empower others to make decisions, while managers tightly control the decision process. In this example, followers who have no control in the decision process also lack motivation to do the job or task. They will do the minimum necessary to keep their jobs because they have no part in the process or end goal. Followers who are involved in the decision-making process are more committed to the task or goal. They will normally do whatever it takes to get it done because they were valued and involved in the process. This is another example of how management stifles the productivity of the business.

Fourth, leaders are proactive, managers are reactive. The proactive leader and his or her followers are always moving forward toward the goal or vision. The manager is focused on the jobs, on followers' mistakes and input. This form of management creates stagnation and wastes time. Bottom line with this approach is that the manager's team will make insufficient progress toward goals. Rather than create solutions to keep moving forward, managers are always stopping to react and correct problems.

Fifth, leaders stimulate right things; most managers monitor wrong things. A lot of managers are monitoring and looking for what the followers are doing wrong, using what they find in the followers' review process. Management by fear is very uninspiring to the follower. The leader, who will be looking to recognize successes and commend positive occurrences, increases morale, production, followers' commitment, and team unity, and improves the culture of the team. Leadership in this instance improves business, while mere management stifles business.

Sixth, leaders are looking for ways of improving initiative and innovation. Managers think of improving compliance and conformance. Leaders are constantly sharing vision with their team. The leader encourages ideas from the team on how to improve, innovate, and achieve the vision. On the other side, a manager is more interested in the team's compliance with rules and conforming to one particular management style. Such a restrictive focus lowers team morale. Followers do not believe they matter. The status quo is maintained, so nothing really improves.

I could point out many other comparisons of the results of leadership versus management, enough to fill many pages, perhaps even another book. My point is how much better both the followers and the business will be with leaders at the helm. With true leadership comes influence, which helps in every aspect of business and life. Leadership improves the culture, morale, commitment level, production, relationships, and many other areas.

Based on the comparisons above, do you see the benefit of leadership over management?

Do you see the value to the business and followers with leadership over management?

Are you willing to change personally to create a culture of leadership and influence over management?

BE-DO-HAVE, NOT HAVE-DO-BE

Most individuals live by the philosophy of HAVE-DO-BE, while the best path to a successful life and becoming the leader you want to be is the BE-DO-HAVE philosophy. As an example of the Have-DO-BE philosophy, when I HAVE a position of authority, I will then DO the things necessary to BE the person I need to be, to become a good leader.

The philosophy used to become a leader is BE-DO-HAVE. Following this philosophy, I will BEcome the person people want to follow. I will continue to DO what is necessary to lead effectively. I will HAVE influence and followers because of who I have become.

> **Leadership is a gift from your followers. To earn it, you must become the person others want to follow.**

By following this concept, leadership and influence come to you. You are not chasing it before you are prepared to have it. The Be-Do-Have philosophy should be used for all aspects of life. It is a stronger path to success as a leader and in life.

What follows is an example of BE-DO-HAVE, from W5 Business Coaching.

A Formula for Life Success
The Art of Being Doing Having

Who must I
Be

What Must I
Do

So That I Can
Have

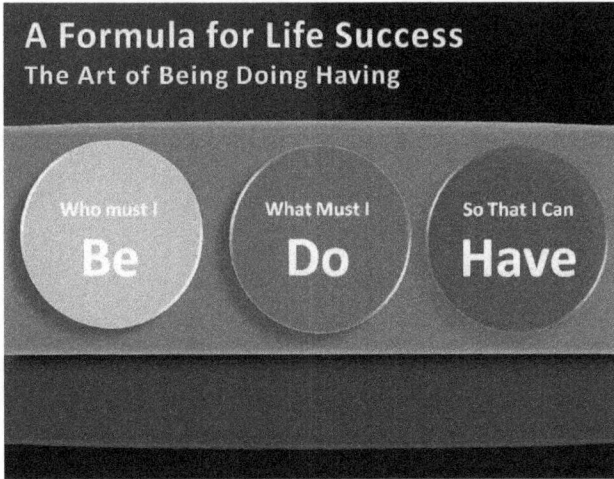

THE PERSON YOU NEED TO BECOME – BE

> Change is a constant in life. Personal development is
> an option. Transforming into the person you need to
> become is a choice.

BECOME A PERSON OF INTEGRITY

Integrity is defined as the quality of being honest and having strong moral principles; moral uprightness; whole or undivided.

The qualities necessary to become a great leader and a person of influence start with integrity. Every relationship is built on trust. Without integrity, there is no trust. Without integrity, there is no respect. Integrity is the cornerstone for leadership and influence. Here's a simple example of integrity. I asked my daughter, Amber McClendon, a high-school teacher, to explain the math term "integer" for me. This is the root word of integrity, and it's been so long since my high-school math days that I needed her help. Amber explained that an integer is a whole number. By extension, then, integrity means living a whole life, an undivided life. This doesn't imply that a leader needs to be perfect. What it does mean, for a leader of integrity, is that, after making an error or saying something untrue, she or he will step up and admit the error or the untruth.

Everyone in today's society feels that he or she has integrity. I have a friend who was in prison, and he told me that even in prison the prisoners feel they have integrity. This being the case, I want to explain what I call small "cracks" that matter to others. I've worked with many people over my career, and quite a few of them were constantly late to meetings. They always had reasons for their tardiness. To them, being late was not a big deal. But to me, this was a small crack in their integrity. To me, time is very important. To me, being late indicates a lack of respect for me and my time.

I know there are a lot of you out there who have run into people like this when you are out and about. At the end of your conversation, you say, "I'll give you a call," or "Let's get together." Then, you never call, and you never get together. I know this seems trivial, and you're probably saying, "What is he talking about?" If a person is willing to tell a small lie it raises the question of whether the same person is willing to tell a big lie. These "cracks" bring doubt into the situation, maybe even a lack of trust. What you think of as a small "crack" may be viewed as a big "crack" to another person.

A good friend of mine, John DiDeminico, works in the construction industry building homes. Last week he was pouring the foundation for a home he's building for himself, and in conversation he mentioned the importance of the integrity of the foundation. John was referring to a foundation without cracks. Even small cracks can become big cracks if they are not filled or taken care of properly. Your word, whether it's arriving on time or following up from a casual comment, represents integrity. Bottom line, integrity is a cornerstone of influence and leadership.

BECOME A TRUSTED PERSON

The verb "trust" means to believe in the reliability, truth, ability, or strength of something. Trust can also be a noun—the quality of trusting. When you are a person of integrity, trusted relationships follow. For you to become a fully trusted leader, your word must be imperative. Being someone your followers can rely on is another important quality for leaders. When you tell your followers you will be there for them, you need to do just that. Followers need to believe that you have the skills and ability necessary to help them in their jobs and that you will be there to help them. Followers must believe that as the leader you have the strength to stand up for them and be there when they need you.

BECOME A POSITIVE PERSON

The word "positive" means a good, affirmative, or constructive quality or attribute; no possibility of doubt, clear, definite.

The attitude of the leader always filters down to the followers. It follows, then, that it's important for the leader to be constructive, affirmative, and a positive example for the followers. This positive attitude creates a culture that fosters innovation, new ideas, increased productivity. In such an environment, people want to come to work. They want to be part of the team. They want to contribute to the team's success. When a leader focuses on positivity instead of negativity, the followers have less fear and feel more freedom to contribute. Followers whose contributions are welcome have higher self-belief, a higher sense of self-worth, and more confidence. Overall, a positive culture makes a very desirable work environment.

As an athlete, I played for coaches who led through both negative and positive reinforcement. I've also worked in corporate America with positive leaders and negative managers. I can tell you that to be a great leader, you need a positive attitude. No one wants to work with or for a negative person. I know all of you have worked in a close environment and have had that negative person in the office. When you see this person coming, you cut your break short or need to use the restroom to get away from that person. If you haven't seen that person in the office, that person might be you. Just kidding! You know what I'm talking about here. Become the leader people respect, the one others want to be around and emulate.

BECOME THE PERSON WHO PUTS OTHERS' INTEREST BEFORE YOUR OWN

When the team wins, the leader wins. A leader who cares about his people will work to help them create their success. Such effort in turn improves the leader's success. This type of leader is looking for ways to improve conditions for the followers. This leader is always looking for better tools, training, and processes to help followers perform more effectively and productively. Positive attention and focus are often characteristic qualities of servant leadership. Putting your followers' interests before your own is very effective in creating security and closeness within the team. This leader's followers are very committed and faithful. This quote by Theodore Roosevelt says it all: "People don't care how much you know until they know how much you care."

BECOME A PERSON OF EXCELLENCE

I know most of you have seen reality television programs showing lifestyles of rich and famous people. When I was young, there was a show called *Life Styles of the Rich and Famous*. The series showcased the lifestyles, cars, yachts, homes, vacations, and appearance of these people. As a kid, I always admired, looked up to, and wanted the lifestyle of these people. Their life of material plenty had an influence on me.

Over the years, though, I've learned that many elements contribute to a life of excellence. Some that I want to touch on are financial success, appearance, philanthropic pursuits, intellectual and personal development, emotional stability, personal balance, and belief systems. Becoming a person of excellence means striving to be the best version of yourself in all areas of your life. We should never settle in life for the mediocre.

> **Everyone has the opportunity to live an extraordinary life. Once you settle for mediocre, that is what your life becomes.**

We should strive for excellence in every aspect of our lives. Having a commitment to excellence builds up and improves your reputation with others. Followers look up to and have a higher level of respect and admiration for people of excellence. As individuals and leaders, we are either attracting people to us or repelling people from us. When you add all this up, it leads to a higher level of influence and leadership.

Financial success is the first area of excellence I want to discuss. When you have had the ability to create financial wealth or achieve a high level of career success, people look up to you. By accomplishing success in these areas, you gain respect. As you reach higher and higher levels, people will seek you out for your thoughts and opinions. Being respected and acknowledged for your achievements does not make you better than anyone else. What it does mean is that you attained a level of success that only the top percentage of the population has attained. The success increases your influence.

Appearance is also very important. Chris Widener writes on p. 92 of *The Art of Influence*, "There are two kinds of impressions: first impressions and lasting impressions." Most of us have also heard the familiar saying "You can't judge a book by its cover," even though judging by first impressions is actually what most people do. Premature judging often happens because of the time constraints of a busy life. I've read that most people have decided whether to allow you to influence them within thirty seconds of meeting and speaking with you. Therefore your appearance truly is important. People see you before they even speak to you, and your appearance is the first thing they judge you on. I'm not saying you need to be a supermodel, but I believe we need to do the best we can with what we have.

Some of the things that contribute to a strong, positive first impression include wearing clean, pressed clothes; being well groomed; appropriate clothing for the event you're attending. Being physically fit is important for your health and self-confidence as well as for a positive appearance. For women, subtle rather than extreme makeup; professional attire that doesn't call attention to itself or is too revealing. For men, especially older men, attend to clipping hair that grows where it's not supposed to grow (nose, ears, neck). Basically, look your best. Even though we say not to judge a book by its cover, in reality we are always being judged.

Philanthropic pursuits are as important as financial success. In the Bible there's a parable that speaks to this point, namely, "to whom much has been given, much will be required." Another quote from the Bible states, "It is more blessed to give than to receive." I believe that while one can be admired for financial success, one is more admired and looked up to for charitable giving. Chris Widener says the same thing in *The Art of Influence*. I know for most people this seems to be difficult. As I became more successful financially, I found charitable areas I felt strongly about and was able to give amounts I was comfortable with. Not only does my giving help the groups I give to, it makes me feel good to be helping others. When I have learned of individuals' giving to charities I've gained additional respect for their contributions and their good hearts.

Intellectual and personal development are needed to continue to improve us as both individuals and leaders. Continuous improvement is what makes us a better version of ourselves. Many people stop the learning process, however, after high school or college. I have some friends who haven't read or listened to a book or experienced training for self-improvement in years, if ever. Leaders are readers! The best leaders and biggest influencers I know continually read and listen to self-improvement books and training.

When you improve yourself intellectually and personally, followers seek you out for advice and counsel. They look up to you and want to emulate you. They are drawn to you because of the confidence and positivity you exude, the knowledge you have gained, and the person you continue to become. Unquestionably, when you have sharpened your saw, you set yourself apart from others, yet most people will not continue to grow, learn, and stretch outside their comfort zone. You will have a huge advantage in the market place if you acquire these skills and do these tasks.

An example of this advantage has been demonstrated by our adult children: Brandon Varnell, Steven Schaefer, Amber McClendon, and Ashley Schaefer. When they were in their late teens, my wife Donna and I asked them all to read several personal development books. We also discussed and shared with them books we'd read and training we'd attended. The perspective they gained has been a big advantage for them. As they joined the work force, they showed significant confidence and maturity during their job interviews and consequently received multiple job offers. In their jobs or areas of expertise, they have excelled, rewarded with income increases and promotions before their peers. As my children continue their intellectual and personal development, I'm confident that their influence, success, and leadership will increase. Becoming a better version of yourself is the best decision you can make for yourself, your personal relationships, and your business relationships. Your leadership and influence with your family and organization will be valued and noted by all.

Mental stability is another area everyone needs to work on and improve on daily. Women tend to do quite well in this area, working continuously on emotional strength and mental stability. They also tend to have very close trusted friends or family members with whom they share problems. Men, however, seem to find it a more difficult area to work on. My own experience was being raised to hold in my problems and not discuss them with others. As a young man, I was told that handling things myself showed strength. But holding back was a misguided habit that stifled my personal growth, success and affiliations. I now understand how important it is to find a mentor with whom to exchange ideas and solve problems.

To manifest emotional strength, you must find a trusted advisor or two and work through challenges or exchange ideas. Working with a trusted advisor on personal and business issues helps you concentrate on what's important and let go of problems over which you have no control. Shifting your focus to those areas you can improve and enhance will relieve stress while increasing productivity. If you can become mentally and emotionally balanced, your leadership and influence with your followers will expand and deepen.

Creating a healthy balance in life is important for your mental health as well as your personal and business relationships. A healthy balance is the result of making family and friends a priority in your life. Something I recognized early in life is the importance and value of time. You've probably heard the old adage from Benjamin Franklin, "Time is money." I believe there's nothing more valuable in this world than time. Think about this: You can always make more money, but when time is lost, you can never get it back. What I'm talking about here is time with your family, friends, and away from work. It's hugely important to stay refreshed, alert, and focused on being your best when leading or working in an organization.

The only way to do this is to take vacation or down time to recharge your mental and physical batteries. My hope for all of you is that you make your families and friends your priority in life. It's imperative to spend quality time with the people you care about and love. Because time is the most valued asset we have, sharing it with those we love shows them they are our top priority. Doing so also relieves us of the mental guilt and stress we would feel if we weren't doing what we needed and wanted to do. Allowing yourself to spend time with family and friends will rekindle relationships and help you to rest your mind, so that you can focus well when you go back to work.

I have many friends who think that not using their vacation makes them a stronger, better employee or leader. If that's your thinking, too, be aware that it is warped. When you don't take a break to recharge, you become less productive, less effective, and more exhausted. You might also become disgruntled about work and less compassionate toward your spouse or partner. Bottom line, you will be more stressed, which could have you in line for a stroke or heart attack. By keeping a balance between work and family, you will have more energy and be more positive toward the important people and events in your life. A positive outlook will increase your influence and attract followers to you. Here's a final thought on the topic from Barbara Bush: "At the end of your life, you will never regret not having passed one more test, not winning one more verdict, or not closing one more deal. You will regret time not spent with a husband, a friend, a child, a parent."

Your belief system, both personal and spiritual, is also important with your followers. It gives them a different view of you and your ability to influence and to lead. I have read the autobiographies of successful people and great leaders who had huge influence, and the majority of them had strong religious beliefs. I'm not here to hit anyone over the head with my Bible. I'm also not saying that you need to get a religion if you don't have one. What I am saying is that a belief system is something many followers look up to, respect, and admire. A belief system gives people a sense of security. If you look back in history, you will find people of huge influence who were also strong in whatever religious belief they practiced, for example, Abraham Lincoln, George Washington, Martin Luther King, Jr., Winston Churchill, Charles de Gaulle, and John F. Kennedy. A number of people in the entertainment industry are known for a strong belief system: Tom Hanks, Ryan Gosling, Stephen Colbert, Elvis Presley, and Carrie Underwood. Such athletes as Stephen Curry have had a strong belief system. Spirituality has been who we are as human beings, important from the beginning of time. When you believe in nothing, you don't have much hope for the world to affect your attitude. Having hope, staying positive, and maintaining balance will make you more attractive and influential to others.

QUALITIES FOR INFLUENCE – Do

There are many qualities that, if we adopt them, will add to our moral and personal fiber. As you **DO** these qualities, you will enhance your business and personal relationships and build your leadership and your influence. These qualities attract followers to you. Without them, you repel would-be followers. Having these qualities makes you a better person, friend, spouse, and leader. The assets I'm referring to include people skills, listening skills, communication skills, and job skills. You also need to be knowledgeable, courageous, honest, visionary, and lead by example. Keep this thought in mind as I expand on these skills and qualities:

> **You must have skills to be a leader.**
> **You need character to be a true influencer.**

PEOPLE SKILLS

In order to become a leader and an influencer, developing your people skills is imperative. You need the ability to deal with different types of people, personalities, ethnic backgrounds, and educational levels, as well as being able to influence these people. Dealing with a variety of people is not easy, but it is possible. As a leader, it is your responsibility to help others see themselves as they could be, for then that is how they will be. With strong people skills, you will gain influence with your followers and be able to help your followers stretch as you lead them. Unless you develop your people skills, you risk remaining a mere manager.

LISTENING SKILLS

Good listening skills may seem like a small thing, but it's an asset that has a big impact on followers. When you, the leader, listen intently and with interest, followers feel a sense of worth. Your followers feel what they say matters. This positive result increases confidence and motivation with your followers. Increasing followers' respect for and confidence in the leader automatically develops committed followers. As a result, the committed team will have higher job satisfaction and will work harder and longer when necessary. They feel their opinions are respected and that they are a part of the process.

> **A leader is more concerned about others than about being interesting.**

Adding listening skills to your tool box will take patience and time, but it will bring mutual rewards for leader and followers.

COMMUNICATION SKILLS

A leader's words breathe life into others, inspiring and motivating them to greater success. Communication skills include spoken and written elements. It is always important to be able to communicate clearly, concisely, and accurately, both in speech and in writing. To others, this ability reflects your level of professionalism and competence. You may not feel that strongly about communication skills, but having good ones is very important to others. When I was a new leader a follower once came up to me after a presentation and said, "You said 'um' twenty-six times during your talk today!" This person was a member of Toastmasters, so proper speaking was important to him. He judged my expertise and intellect by that one presentation. After that encounter, I worked on this skill until I became a professional speaker. In memos I've sent, I've also had feedback from followers correcting my grammar. I have a masters' degree in business administration, so I'm not ignorant, but my grammar and spelling are definitely not perfect, so I've worked on improving this skill as well. I often use Microsoft spell-check for spelling, and as often as possible I have my wife, Donna, check my grammar as well. So, if you recognize there is some area with room for improvement, you'll be wise to work on stretching your skills and using available tools. You never know who is listening to you and reading your materials, and making a positive impact is important.

JOB SKILLS AND KNOWLEDGE

One thing is of utmost important for a great leader: you must have job skills and the knowledge necessary for the job or position you're in. Without those skills and knowledge, you won't be able to answer questions, help, or train followers. With great job skills and knowledge, however, a leader can help followers reach the success they desire. Influence grows as the leader impacts the team with knowledge and skills.

COURAGE

Courage is a virtue that strengthens all the other virtues. Aristotle called courage the first virtue, because it makes all other virtues possible. Courage, in my opinion, is one of the most important human virtues. If you think about this, without courage leadership would be weak and wither. In business and sales, there will be no success unless you have the courage to take calculated risks. In sales, you need courage to ask for the business.

A leader with courage will make bold decisions but reasoned judgement. Leaders with courage are normally humble yet confident. Courage allows leaders to be decisive. Using a baseball analogy, they are willing to step up to the plate and take a swing. A leader with courage is there for the followers, encouraging them to take risks. A leader has faith in the followers and empowers them by letting go of control. With courage, a leader will also be strong enough to give tough feedback when needed.

HONESTY

I found a good discussion of honesty by Kouzes and Posner in *Boundless Management,* Boundless, 26 May. Honesty refers to different aspects of moral character. It indicates positive and virtuous attributes such as integrity, truthfulness, and straightforwardness. Honesty is essential to a leader's legitimacy, credibility, and ability to develop trust with followers. Honesty is a quality that adds more glue to your credibility, trust, and truthfulness. You need honesty in what you say, how you act, and what you do. Honesty is an attribute. If you don't stay true with your honesty, it affects your integrity. In essence, honesty is part of your moral character and a portion of your integrity.

VISION

As far back as biblical times, leaders have spoken of the importance of vision, for example, chapter 29, verse 18 in the book of Proverbs: "Where there is no vision, the people perish." Great leaders have a clear, specific, and defined view of where the company or their teams are going. Leaders who have true influence are able to gain their followers' commitment to accomplish the vision. When leaders believe strongly and passionately in their vision, it feeds down to their followers. In many cases, these followers will choose working and accomplishing the vision over other options.

Jack Welch, former CEO of General Electric, has an excellent view of vision: "Good business leaders create vision, articulate the vision, passionately own the vision, and, relentlessly, drive it to completion." Having or creating a vision for your team is very important. A great vision will help a leader recruit better employees, because successful people want to work for a leader with great vision. They also want to work for a company that has a strong, clear vision and knows where it's going. To be a leader, you need to know where you want the company to go, where you are going, and where your team is going. This quality adds to your respect, confidence, and influence with your followers.

LEAD BY EXAMPLE AND FROM THE FRONT

> **A leader can't lead others where he or she is unwilling to go to or hasn't yet been.**

You need to be a shining example of what you want from others. The characteristics you exhibit will influence your followers as the team emulates you. Every great leader I've ever worked for, read about, or watched in my life has always led from the front, just as I do. They don't ask their followers to do anything they haven't done or wouldn't do. Leading by example creates a tremendous amount of respect, admiration, and commitment from followers.

> **Leadership is showing people what you expect, not just telling them.**

When you look back in history at great leaders, you will find this characteristic. You can find this is true of leaders from the military, social, political, and athletic arenas of life. When you look at such a leader as Napoleon Bonaparte, you read that he charged ahead of his men. To protect him, his men charged faster and harder. During World War II, John F. Kennedy saved his men by his own heroism. His strength kept his men hopeful and alive. Martin Luther King, Jr., led his marches and protests in the front of the crowd. Michael Jordan, with his extreme work ethic in practice, in the gym and on the court, pushed his teammates to realize their highest potential.

Leading by example is a quality of all great leaders. Remember that leadership is a gift from your followers. To earn it, you must become the person others want to follow. Remember, if you're in the background just telling followers what to do, you're a manager, not a leader. Carl Golden wrote on this topic, "Good leaders must lead by example. By walking your talk, you become a person others want to follow. When leaders say one thing, but do another, they erode trust—a critical element of productive leadership. My suggestion is to lead by example and from the front and you will gain respect, admiration and Influence."

ABILITY TO EMPOWER FOLLOWERS

As a manager, you maintain control of most aspects of the followers' job, tasks, and responsibilities. You monitor every step taken and look for failures by the followers. Empowering your followers is a clear sign of a leader. A true leader has trained followers appropriately, has confidence and faith in followers to complete the job and tasks effectively and successfully. As a leader, when your followers know you have confidence and faith in them, they will normally do more than expected to maintain your confidence. They will be willing to go above and beyond for their leader, because they feel they are part of the process and have control of their success.

The leader does, however, have checks and balances on progress and success. When retraining or retooling is necessary, the follower is part of the process. Involving the team in a training system supports continuous improvement. The process also prepares followers for their chance at leadership.

HUMILITY

Humility is very misunderstood as an important leadership characteristic. The leadership qualities we more often think of are passion, decisiveness, drive, risk-taking, and perfectionism, to name a few. So why is humility so important? How does humility add to a leader's strength and influence? While many see humility as a weakness, not a strength, on the contrary, humility enhances the leader's strength and influence in many ways.

In *Executive Ethics: Ethical Dilemmas and Challenges for the C-Suite*, Scott A. Quataro and Robert R. Sims wrote on p. 80, "Next, we consider where proper humility stems from, the worldview and core values genesis of leadership. At the heart of our argument is the exploration of five key ideas that from our experience define leadership in action attributes–fallibility, vulnerability, transparency, inadequacy, and interdependency. Leaders who develop a comfort level with these five key abilities are those who engender loyalty from their followers and find long-term effectiveness in leadership."

When higher-level followers have ambitions of promotion to a leadership position, they sometimes have difficulty changing their mindset in regard to the importance of humility. While such people may have many of the leadership qualities we've mentioned, some lack humility. Leaders often condition followers toward achieving goals, being the best, being self-confident, being perfect. It is a leader's responsibility to prepare followers for leadership, which also includes humility.

A leader who is overconfident, believing he or she knows it all, and expects perfection makes it very difficult for followers to look up to, respect, and admire her or him. I've found that it's very important for a leader to be able to admit personal faults. Followers don't expect leaders to be perfect. They do expect them to be honest, trustworthy, transparent, and have integrity. Humility in a leader allows followers to see that their leader is a real person and not perfect. An appropriately humble leader will earn more respect, admiration, and loyalty from followers. Remember, humility is a big strength in leadership, not a weakness. Humility shows the team that its leader is human.

CONFIDENCE

A leader can be taught or trained in many skills, among them problem-solving, coaching, mentoring, and job knowledge. Confidence needs to be developed. It comes with accomplishments and successes. I believe that success breeds more success, with successes building self-confidence. As a leader, confidence is more important than any skill. Without confidence, you won't be decisive. You will second-guess yourself. You may have job knowledge but lack the confidence on how and when to use that knowledge. It takes confidence to lead others to fulfill the vision of the company and their own personal vision of success. Self-confidence is a character trait and a very valuable asset. When someone is qualified for a position of leadership by the necessary skills and job knowledge but lacks the essential confidence in self, her or his own abilities, and vision, others will not follow. And if you don't have people following you, you're just going for a walk.

The value of confidence in leaders is that it builds trust and confidence with followers. A leader's confidence also increases confidence in the followers. If your confidence is growing, followers' confidence grows as well. To gain more self-confidence, look at your own success and accomplishments. In a blog I came across from Peter Barron Stark entitled "The role confidence plays in leadership," the author states that leaders with confidence are happier, more motivated, build better relationships, are open to risk taking, accept constructive feedback, and think for themselves. He included this excellent quote from Francisco Dao: "Self-confidence is the fundamental basis for which leadership grows. Trying to teach leadership without first building confidence is like building a house on a foundation of sand. It may have a nice coat of paint, but it is ultimately shaky at best."

If you build up your self-confidence and thus the confidence of your followers, your relationship and trust with your followers will also grow. My book *Belief: The Foundation to Success* is a great reference tool for self-belief, self-confidence, and overall success.

DECISIVENESS

Decisiveness, the ability to review information and make a solid quick decision, is a valuable asset and skill to leaders. Yet decisiveness is an area where most leaders fail. Often, when leaders request more and more information to analyze, they get analysis paralysis. Leaders who normally do this have a fear of failure. The interesting thing is that by not making a decision, the leader fails anyway.

It takes courage and confidence to make decisions. The only way to gain courage and confidence is to take action. Taking action and creating success builds more confidence. Leaders must be willing to make a decision with the minimal amount of information available. They must also be flexible enough to deal with any imperfections that arise as the decision is implemented. Making decisions quickly shows followers you have the necessary confidence and willingness to move ahead.

> **Be decisive! Indecision makes life unstable and prevents us from moving forward.**

Being decisive increases the level of commitment and trust in your followers. It is imperative for a leader to be decisive.

Chapter 4

THE EFFECT OF LEADERSHIP VERSUS MANAGEMENT ON FOLLOWERS – THE HAVE

E arlier in this book I discussed a process called Be-Do-Have, as opposed to how most people work, which is Have-Do-Be. In the process I'm referring to, you should become better; then, you work harder to become more. Bottom line, who you BEcome is the first thing you do. Then, you'll DO something to HAVE something.

Here's an example of how it works. I will BEcome the person people want to follow; I will continue to DO what is necessary to lead effectively. I will then HAVE influence with followers because of who I BEcame. By following the Be-Do-Have process, leadership and influence come to you. In this chapter, we'll discuss what you will HAVE by living through this process.

MANAGEMENT

Many people are just managers instead of leaders. Some of you will look at the information I present here and say, "Oh, that isn't me. I don't do that." If you asked your followers, though, and they gave you an honest answer, you might learn you are actually a manager. In order for you to create progress and advancement, improvement and change will be imperative. You must first acknowledge where you are in the process. Second, you must be willing to change, improve, and be the person you need to become to lead and influence.

The first area affected by management is productivity. A manager who monitors every aspect of the process stifles productivity by slowing most things down. First, the followers are not given the opportunity to express their individual views as to how the job gets done. The manager keeps very tight control of the job and process. The unstated feeling is that things either will be done the manager's way, or you can hit the highway. This is managing by fear, and it stifles creativity, productivity, and individuality. This style causes productivity to suffer, and in the long run the business will suffer as well.

The resultant disadvantage is lack of business growth. Stifling an individual follower's productivity has a negative effect on overall company profits and production. If the culture, philosophy, or style of the business is one of management instead of leadership, future leadership within the company will also be stifled. In order to improve or change, the business will need to change internally. The top leadership team needs to change the culture from that of management to leadership. In this situation, the management team would benefit from personal development training to make the shift in mindset. There is often pushback from current managers, however, because they don't like change.

Change your thinking, change your world.

If the pushback is too strong, it may become necessary to replace managers who are unwilling to change. If the managers are not willing to make the shift to leaders, they may have a negative attitude towards the company and the followers and could become a negative influence in the organization. This negativity will stifle the business growth even more. I suggest that when changes of culture must occur, first get buy-in from the manager, then the followers. Here's my view on change that may help in the process:

> **Change is a constant in life, personal development is an option.** Transforming into the person you need to become is a choice.

In a management-driven culture, managers may be afraid that if they train their followers too well, they will be replaced. Replacing yourself only happens if you don't improve, develop, and continue to grow as a positive leader. If you don't progress into leadership, you stifle your own advancement and your followers' opportunity. In order to capture the qualities and characteristics needed to create leadership and influence for higher levels of advancement, again, you must progress into leadership by moving out of the managerial role. Remember my quote: "Change your thinking; change your world." Your refusal to change hurts you and your business.

As a leader in corporate America, I learned great lessons about leadership and advancement. My goal was to hire people who had the skills to replace me. I hired the best I could find. In doing so, I made a great decision, because my hires were high achievers, and their achievement made me look great as their leader. As I trained them, they then developed in to leaders and were promoted to leadership positions. By following this process, I too was promoted every eighteen to twenty-four months to a higher level of leadership. Our strong team strengthened the company, its leadership structure, and its production. By holding to this mindset and process throughout my corporate career, it took me to the C-Level of a privately held company that I ran for five years.

Remember, when you remain a manager, you lack the knowledge, expertise, skills, confidence, qualities, or ability needed to help your followers become leaders. You stifle your followers' opportunity to advance and lead others within your company or with another company. If you are looking to advance but don't have a leader assisting you, you should find a mentor or coach or start your own personal development program. You should read books, listen to trainings or audios, and create an action plan for development. This process is difficult for most people, because the studying requires extra time and effort above and beyond their current job.

Businesses rise and fall on leadership. Without an influx and development of capable new leaders, any business will wither. With new leaders, individuals can improve personally and professionally. New leaders also improve possibilities for building business and personal relationships. You can improve every aspect of your life as you grow as a leader. I suggest that rather than remaining a manager, you make a decision to develop yourself into a leader with influence.

Do you want to become a better version of you?

Do you want to become a leader instead of a manager?

Are you ready to start a personal development program to become a leader and true influencer?

Are you ready to find and work with a coach or mentor to develop into a leader?

LEADERSHIP

For those of you who consider yourselves leaders and true influencers, this section of the book will be a reinforcement of what you already know to be true. As a true leader and influencer, you also know that reinforcement of solid principles, ideas, and teaching is foundational to your continued success.

You also know that you can read or hear the same or similar information time and again, but it doesn't affect you until you're ready to receive it. "When the student is ready, the teacher will appear" is an old saying sometimes attributed to the Buddha. I can't tell you how many times I've re-read the same books, listened to the same trainings, and attended the same speaker's seminar and come away with new ideas I can apply or new information I can use. So the improvements and increases I will touch on here will be no surprise to you who are already leaders. To those of you who are still managers, however, this material will be unknown and a surprise to you.

Leadership and influence can be linked to many improvements and increases. Productivity is an easy one to recognize. Followers who have more control of their success and participation in a process become happier, though they do need clear direction and a clear vision of where they need to go. The followers will become more accountable to their leader and want to maintain the leader's trust and respect. When they are happier, they are willing to do more on the job, which increases their productivity.

A leader has the ability to empower followers by increasing the followers' independence and ability to make decisions, allowing them to control their own destiny. With this increase in control comes greater self-confidence, sense of self-worth, self-respect, and respect for their peers. All these mindset improvements bring a desire to do their best for you as their leader. This increase in your followers' independence both improves the company productivity and prepares the follower for leadership.

As the leader, when you empower your followers, it substantially increases their motivation in many different ways. It increases their motivation to do a better job; it increases their ideas for improving the process; it increases their motivation to improve themselves. All of these positive increases help the company, the leader, and the followers.

Growth into leadership and influence will also increase followers' level of commitment. Followers who feel empowered with greater control, independence, and self-value will have a huge commitment level for the company, the leader, and their job. With this commitment level comes a willingness to voluntarily work harder and longer. Followers will have higher job satisfaction, higher motivation, and higher loyalty, all of which creates longevity with the company. Let me emphasize again: When a leader empowers the team, the consequent higher commitment level helps and improves the company, the leader, and the follower.

With increased motivation comes an increase in loyalty to the leader first, the job second, and the company last. In other words, it creates a strong bond between the follower and leader. This bond carries through to the job performance and to the followers' desire to stay with the company longer. Empowered followers have hope and the opportunity for upward mobility because of their improvement, development, and performance.

A situation with no possibility of upward mobility kills all the possibilities for increases and improvement we've discussed. But when leaders develop, mentor, lead, and properly train their followers, an increase in their opportunity for advancement occurs. Even if there are no opportunities with the current company or business, prepared and properly trained employees can earn a promotion with another company. I've known many followers who continued to work with a particular leader solely so they could develop into and become better leaders. Even if this occurs to you as a leader, you have the follower for an extended period of time, taking advantage of their production and expertise while she or he is with you. As leaders, we need to be there for our followers to improve, develop, and train them to become the best they can become.

Chapter 5

LASTING BENEFITS OF TRUE LEADERSHIP AND INFLUENCE

There are many lasting benefits to working on and developing yourself into a person of influence. The personal development you do will help you in every aspect of your life. You will become a better spouse, parent, salesperson, business person, leader, and overall version of yourself. You will have the ability to influence everyone you come into contact with.

The first lasting benefit to consider is the culture created when great character, leadership, and influence lead the way. This culture is one of mutual respect. The leader listens to and gives value to the followers. Because of this leader's example of respect, followers emulate it and share it among themselves. Mutual respect breeds confidence within the followers, and confidence leads to the courage to share new ideas. This culture also allows for an open policy to implement new ideas. The respect, courage, and confidence give followers the push they need to take the calculated risks necessary for the business to grow and progress, as well as for individual followers. Such a culture improves the process and increases results.

Another lasting benefit of this culture is the big impact on each individual's results, which then improves the company's results. Employees are more positive when their voices are heard and they are involved in the process. When problems arise, they are quick to find solutions. When something is not working, they have the confidence to speak out and make changes when necessary to correct the problem. They are more focused on better results, which allows them to produce those results. Even though they are focused, they remain flexible so that they can change direction when necessary. All of this is positive and a direct result of leadership.

As a leader you are only as good as the team you put together. When you have a positive, motivating culture with a clear vision, it attracts better followers. Once you, the leader, share your vision, your leadership philosophy, and your processes, people will want to be part of your team. As a leader, this gives you a larger pool to choose followers from and brings a higher level of talent to your team and the company. Employee recruiting and retention is one of the biggest keys to the success of your team and company. Becoming an influential leader and implementing this type of culture is the key to accomplishing longer retention and bringing in the best talent. This maintains the cohesive efforts of the team and allows your followers to reach higher levels of success, which again improves the results of the company. Hiring and training new employees is a major cost to a company. A new employee's production is low until he or she is up to speed, so improving retention directly affects the financial bottom line.

A group of followers who work under a manager's control and fear normally will not do anything extra to get the job done. In fact, they usually will not volunteer, and if asked will help grudgingly. In this circumstance, the job will probably take longer and may not be completed up to the standard desired. But with a leader who exemplifies the level of influence we have been discussing, team members are willing to go above and beyond, and in most cases willing to do so voluntarily. They are focused on completing the vision, right along with the leader, because of their respect and admiration for the influential leader.

This happens because the leader has created a culture giving followers a part in the process. The leader has created a cohesive unit that uses teamwork, team sharing, and team ideas and interaction to accomplish the vision. The followers are willing to share information with one another. They are competitive to win as a team, not compete one against another for individual status. The goal here is success of the whole, not the individual. As John F. Kennedy said, "A rising tide lifts all boats." This is true in business and in all aspect of our lives. True leadership, influence, and mutual respect, create this culture of a cohesive group and success.

Another huge lasting benefit that supports longevity with the company is development of a team of leaders. With managing, followers do not grow, make decisions, or come up with ideas to improve processes. Followers do things because they have to, not because they want to. They have no hope of advancement, because the manager doesn't provide the necessary mentoring, training, or support. By becoming a true leader who has influence, you develop more leaders. They follow the mentorship example of the leader. They look up to the leader. They respect the leader. And, most important, because the leader has influence with them, they want to do well so as not to disappoint the leader. Providing independence, training, and mentorship, leaders with influence create a continuous stream of leaders for the company and for their teams.

I'm sure you can see the many benefits of having followers who are able and willing to lead in your absence, willing to lead individual projects, and willing to lead by example. In this situation, decisions get made based on the vision and training to keep things always moving forward. Most managers hire people who may be good but not great. A manager doesn't want to be challenged by an up-and-coming leader. Such a manager wants to hire people who do what they're told, when they're told, and how to do it. Such managers don't want to be replaced or passed up by their own people. My advice is to become the leader you need to be and hire people who can take your place. They will make you and your team more successful. They will raise the bar for the rest of the team. They will be there when you need them. Most important, by building other leaders, you will be promoted to a position of more responsibility. You will not regret it.

The final lasting benefit I want to point out is respect. As a leader with influence, you are building a culture of open communication and respect for all ideas, opinions, and people. When everyone, every idea and opinion is respected, it brings confidence to your followers. This new confidence brings out ideas and opinions that you would otherwise not hear. This respect for all team members grows and becomes the culture for each individual. Respect fosters a more cohesive team, a more productive team; a more motivated and happier team. Everyone wants to be valued and respected. When you bring respect to your followers and foster a culture of mutual respect, you will be amazed at the increase in production, improved attitude of the followers, great ideas generated, and ultimate success of each individual and the entire team.

Chapter 6

THE BENEFITS TO YOUR PERSONAL LIFE AND RELATIONSHIPS

T his chapter starts where the last one ended—with respect. In life, whether we're talking about business or personal respect, it is necessary to build relationships. When you develop yourself and your character personally to become a person of influence, you become a respected leader in every aspect of your life, both personally and professionally.

Let's consider the impact you make to those in your personal life. For those of you with children, you become a better version of you. You are the person your children look up to and want to emulate. I know that you are all saying that your children do this now. I'm very sure they do. Since that is true, isn't it our responsibility to be the best example for them that we can be? By continuing to work on becoming a better version of yourself and improving the character traits we have discussed in this book, you become an even better example for your family. If you really want your children to grow up and become an asset to society, then you must first become the person you want them to be.

For those of you with a significant other or friends you care about, the same concept also applies to your dealings with them. You will treat people around you according to the person that you are in that moment. If you want to treat your spouse, significant other, and friends with respect and admiration, then you must work on yourself to become someone worthy of respect and admiration. Your character and attitude determine how you treat those around you. No matter who you are, you can always improve yourself. Improving yourself will give you a greater respect for everyone around you. And when you give respect, you will receive respect in return. Treating those around you with respect in your personal life builds closer relationships with them.

When you improve and become that better version of yourself, not only do the people closest to you have more respect for you, they want to be around you more. When you become a better leader and person, more people will be attracted to you. The people in your personal life will be more open and transparent with you. They will have more confidence in you. You will be a more positive influence on those around you. As most of you know, no one wants to be around negative people or negative influences. All these things build closer more meaningful relationships. You become the leader in your personal relationships.

This will also bring a higher quality of individuals into your personal life. This is very important for you personally but even more so for your overall success in life. I have been blessed to have many very high-level personal friends. I believe this is because of who I am as a person. These high-level and successful individuals have been a guiding light for me in business and in my personal life. They have contributed to my success personally and in business. There is nothing better than having people in your life you can look up to, admire, and get advice from. Your success is partly determined by your affiliations. When you become a higher-quality leader and person, you attract a higher quality of people personally and in business. This equates to a higher level of success and happiness in life.

You become a role model. By becoming a better person and leader, you become a role model to those around you. Because of the concepts I've covered in this book and in my first book, *Belief: The Foundation to Success*, many people have asked me to mentor or coach them. When you become a better version of yourself, everyone around you will have a higher level of respect for you; they will look up to you and admire you. You have become the person they want to be. You have become a role model. Continue working on yourself and you will continue to become a better version of you. You then continue to be a better role model for everyone around you.

Chapter 7

THOUGHTS AND CONCLUSIONS

I was very passionate about writing this book and the information that I shared with you. This book will allow you to make a choice and decision to move forward from manager to leader as well as develop into a stronger leader. If you are currently a leader, you can make a decision to continue to develop and improve to a higher level of leadership. As you reach higher levels of leadership, you can add some of the attributes you may not currently possess. You can also add some of the other leadership styles to your current style. This development will give you the ability to lead a larger and more diverse group of followers. It also gives you true influence with your peers and followers, as well as in your business relationships, personal leaderships, and with other leaders.

This book gives you a clear explanation and view of the different management styles and leadership styles. I did this to allow each of you to compare whether you are currently a manager or leader. I added a description of each style to allow each of you an opportunity to look internally to see what style you fit into. My main goal is for each of you to be able to analyze and figure out where you are and where you want to go. It allows you to honestly figure out who you are, decide where you are currently.and if you are either a manager or leader.

Throughout this book, I have talked about management, leadership, and influence. The main truth I wanted to convey is the importance of leadership in business and in your personal life. I also want you to know that anyone can become a leader with influence. In fact, there are leaders all around you. Some of them may be teachers, coaches, firemen, police officers, or pastors. You may find them in the military. They could even be entry-level employees who their peers look up to. Here's the key to leadership that I want to emphasize: The stronger character qualities you have and develop, the more influence you gain. The more influence you have with the people around you, the higher level of leadership you possess. Don't get me wrong, you need the necessary skills for the job, but without character, you cannot lead or gain influence.

I believe that if you have read this book, you are interested in growing and developing yourself to a higher level of leadership. If you are currently a manager, you can develop into a leader. As a leader, you can develop into a higher level of leadership. The higher the level of leadership you attain, the more influence you will have with your peers, followers, and in your business and personal relationships. If you use this information honestly, you will figure out where you are as a manager or a leader. In order to know where you are going and be able to move forward, you must know and acknowledge where you are starting from. This will also give you the opportunity to decide where you want to develop yourself. By analyzing and applying this information and creating new habits daily, you can advance to any level of leadership and influence that you want to achieve.

I have also shared interviews of high-level leaders or up-and-coming leaders. As you read these interviews and compared the qualities that each leader possessed, I'm sure you noted the similarities among them. I have noted these similarities in every leader I've worked for and with. This further proves my theory about the importance of character in leadership. In fact, as you look at them further, you will see that of the different leaders interviewed, the higher the level they've attained in business and life, the more character qualities they possess and the more leadership styles they use in their leadership. Over time they've continued to develop and improve their character and increase their leadership styles.

If you don't agree with my analysis and decide not to improve, develop, or change into a leader, that will be your decision and choice. It is my opinion that you will remain a manager. You can have some success as a manager, but you will not be able to attain massive success personally or with your team. This means that you and your team will remain average or below average at your current position. This creates stress and fear of possible job loss (lack of production) from your leaders as well as the threat of your followers taking your job. You have the decision and choice to change this by changing your mindset, developing yourself personally, and changing your style and habits to those of leadership instead of management.

In Chapter Five, I discussed the lasting benefits of influence, leadership, and developing leaders. I also pointed out many benefits for the companies you work for, such as development of other leaders, inspiration and motivation for your followers, increased production, and improved business and personal relationships. The biggest lasting benefit is the influence you will have in every aspect of your life. I say that influence is the biggest benefit because when you have true influence with those around you, it improves every aspect of your life in business and personally. People around you will admire you, respect you, look to you for advice, like you, work harder for you, want to be around you, and willingly to go above and beyond for you. You will impact and develop others to the point where they will continue your legacy with others as they grow into leaders. This is all excellent!

In conclusion, you have nothing to lose and everything to gain, by growing and developing yourself. I know that some of you will say you don't have time. Some of you will say you don't think you need to improve. Some of you will say you're not sure it's worth the effort. I want to address these excuses and any others you may come up with. Here is something for you to think about:

> **When you develop yourself on the inside,
> it changes things on the outside.**

You can make excuses, or you can change and create success by becoming a better version of yourself. First of all, what can be better than becoming a better person? This makes you a better parent, spouse, significant other, friend, peer, and leader. What could be better than that? Some of the changes are decisions to become a person with the qualities we've talked about. Then you need to practice those qualities every day. The character qualities need to become who you are, not just words and definitions.

Following are the answers for those of you that say you have no time. You can listen to CDs or audios in your car while driving. Most of you drive an hour or more per day to work and back. With this much time in a year or two, you would have a PhD in personal development or leadership. Maybe you're in sales and in and out of your car all day. In this case you could have that PhD sooner. There are many audio books, seminars, and trainings that you can read, listen to, or attend. The seminars and trainings would take additional personal time to attend outside of work. To help you develop, there are coaching calls you can listen to in real time or recorded; listen during your drive time. You can hire a personal business coach to help you develop as a leader. There are many ways and many choices to get you where you want to go as a leader.

> **Only you can ensure that you become the person you need to be** to get to where you want to go in life.

The key is to make a decision that you want to improve. Then decide what level you want to reach. From there, create a plan, either by yourself or with the help of a leader, mentor, or coach. Last but not least, take action on the plan every day. Make personal development an everyday habit. By doing this, you will have continuous improvement. You will improve a little bit every day, and before you know it, you will become a person of high influence.

Suggested Readings or Audios

This list of suggested books or audios should get you started:

The Art of Influence, The Angel Inside, and *Twelve Pillars* by Chris Widener

The Travelers Gift and *The Final Summit* by Andy Andrews

How to Win Friends and Influence People by Dale Carnegie

Go for No by Richard Fenton and Andrew Waltz

Go Givers Sell More by Bob Burg

The Book on Mind Management by Dennis R. Deaton

Above the Rim by NBA star Joe Courtney

5 Levels of Leadership, Developing the Leader Within You, Developing the Leaders Around You, and 15 *Invaluable Laws of Growth, Failing Forward* by John Maxwell

Relentless Success by Todd Stottlemyre.

Belief: The Foundation to Success by Gary Varnell

TOOLS AND THOUGHTS

I also have some tools and information to help you on your leadership journey. The first one is the top ten motivators for your followers, Source: Leigh Valley Business 7/17/2013 and Rapid Learning Institute, John Costello, May 8, 2009

TOP TEN MOTIVATORS AT WORK

1. Full appreciation (recognition) for work well done, expressed directly by leaders personally and publicly.
2. Learning and career development and advancement opportunities.
3. Decision making authority and autonomy (empower them).
4. Flexible working hours, arrangements, and dress code.
5. Being kept informed about work issues and having the opportunity to give input before policy is made (mutual respect)
6. Exciting and meaningful work, and the sense of making a difference.
7. Working with great people.
8. A nice leader who criticizes constructively and disciplines fairly.

9. Management support, time, and help.
10. Fair pay and compensation.

The second thing I want to share is on human relations: Source: by Peter Borner 4,27,2012 in Business Leadership.

A Short Course in Leader Follower Relations
The six most important words – I admit that I was wrong.
The five most important words – You did a great job.
The four most important words – What do you think?
The three most important words – Could you please…
The two most important words – Thank you!
The most important word – We
The least important word – I

The last thing I want to share with all of you is a leadership test. This test will help you evaluate where you are in your leadership journey. It will also point out where you need to improve or change. Source John E Lang, CEO Pinnacle Development Group, LLC.

THE LEADERSHIP FACTOR

Effective leaders seem to have one quality in common. Effective leadership can make you more imaginative, more creative, more powerful, and ultimately more successful. This quiz will help you assess your current leadership factor. You then can make improvements.

Simply circle the best and most honest answer. When you are finished, look at the scoring instruction for your personal assessment

1) I have a vision on where we are going and set long-term goals.

A) always B) most of the time C) sometimes D) not often E) never

2) My actions align with my major defined purpose.

A) always B) most of the time C) sometimes D) not often E) never

3) In a stressful situation, I remain calm and maintain my status as an effective leader.

A) always B) most of the time C) sometimes D) not often E) never

4) I have a vision on where we are going and set short-term goals.

A) always B) most of the time C) sometimes D) not often E) never

5) I take delight in complimenting people that I work with when progress is made.

A) always B) most of the time C) sometimes D) not often E) never

6) I know what is required of an effective leader, and whenever possible, I concentrate on my actions to assess what areas I can improve.

A) always B) most of the time C) sometimes D) not often E) never

7) I have a deep-rooted understanding of the functions of my organization.

A) always B) most of the time C) sometimes D) not often E) never

8) I find it easy to be the cheerleader for others, when times are good and when times are bad.

A) always B) most of the time C) sometimes D) not often E) never

9) Looking back over the quality of my leadership in stressful situations, I regret some of my actions.

A) always B) most of the time C) sometimes D) not often E) never

10) People often look up to me and my values.

A) always B) most of the time C) sometimes D) not often E) never

11) I admit my mistakes and take responsibility for my actions

A) always B) most of the time C) sometimes D) not often E) never

12) I accept complete responsibility for myself and everything that happens in my life.

A) always B) most of the time C) sometimes D) not often E) never

13) Rather than simply react to whatever comes into my life, I try to take a leadership role in those events.

A) always B) most of the time C) sometimes D) not often E) never

14) Team accomplishment is more important to me than my own personal accomplishments.

A) always B) most of the time C) sometimes D) not often E) never

15) When a co-worker is rude to me, I feel hurt and try to solve the conflict.

A) always B) most of the time C) sometimes D) not often E) never

16) I can separate the important issues from inconsequential ones.

A) always B) most of the time C) sometimes D) not often E) never

17) I am not fazed by failures as I believe that failure offers an opportunity for hard work and determination

A) always B) most of the time C) sometimes D) not often E) never

18) I like to challenge myself to surpass the targets that I set for myself.

A) always B) most of the time C) sometimes D) not often E) never

19) I have counseled employees who have personal problems (family, health, financial).

A) always B) most of the time C) sometimes D) not often E) never

20) I am usually the one to take initiative for anything new or unusual.

A) always B) most of the time C) sometimes D) not often E) never

21) I do not give up on things easily and like to finish what I have started.

A) always B) most of the time C) sometimes D) not often E) never

22) I am adaptable to change and am able to adjust to new people and new ideas.

A) always B) most of the time C) sometimes D) not often E) never

23) I am a champion of change.

A) always B) most of the time C) sometimes D) not often E) never

24) I seek out mentors and coaches to teach me and mentor me.

A) always B) most of the time C) sometimes D) not often E) never

25) When I am in control of my emotions, I choose to be happy

A) always B) most of the time C) sometimes D) not often E) never

26) I take time to relax and regenerate in my life.

A) always B) most of the time C) sometimes D) not often E) never

27) I associate myself with confident, successful-minded people.

A) always B) most of the time C) sometimes D) not often E) never

28) I am good at multitasking and can simultaneously yet efficiently perform many tasks at once.

A) always B) most of the time C) sometimes D) not often E) never

29) I find pleasure in recognizing and celebrating the accomplishments of others.

A) always B) most of the time C) sometimes D) not often E) never

30) I manage to make people feel involved in the decisions when discussing an issue.

A) always B) most of the time C) sometimes D) not often E) never

31) I can separate the personal issues from business ones.

A) always B) most of the time C) sometimes D) not often E) never

32) I have complete integrity and can be trusted.

A) always B) most of the time C) sometimes D) not often E) never

33) I am a good delegator.

A) always B) most of the time C) sometimes D) not often E) never

34) I can make a presentation to a group of peers with confidence.

A) always B) most of the time C) sometimes D) not often E) never

35) I know how to sell.

A) always B) most of the time C) sometimes D) not often E) never

36) I admit my mistakes and take responsibility for my actions.

A) always B) most of the time C) sometimes D) not often E) never

37) When involved in group projects, I frequently find myself to be an "idea generator."

A) always B) most of the time C) sometimes D) not often E) never

38) I accept the world the way it really is, not how I wish it was, hope it to be, and want it to be.

A) always B) most of the time C) sometimes D) not often E) never

39) I like myself.

A) always B) most of the time C) sometimes D) not often E) never

******Scoring Instructions******

Add up number of "A" answers and multiply by 4 = _____

Add up number of "B" answers and multiply by 3 = _____

Add up number of "C" answers and multiply by 2 = _____

Add up number of "D" answers and multiply by 1 = _____

Add up number of "E" answers and multiply by 0 = _____

140 to 160 Points: You have a strong, solid factor of effective leadership. People follow you, and feel proud of doing so. Leading people is what you are born to do. Diplomacy, humility, honesty, commitment, and competence are all what you have and what you work with. You make decisions decisively and are ready to accept responsibility if things do not go well. Accepting responsibility should be one of your biggest assets if you want to lead people. In life, you can either be a goal setter or a problem solver. If you are problem solvers, the world controls your agenda as you react to it. Strong leaders are goal setters, and control their own destiny and the world becomes their canvas. Share the credit and bear the liability alone. You have all the qualities that are required to be a good leader, both in attitude and in work. As a leader, you have posture and confidence. Strong leaders have an abundant mentality and people want a piece of your value and power. When you demonstrate posture, you will find that the world will beat a path to your doorstep and automatically pursue an association with you. Be congenial to all and you will see yourself reaching the stars with your team following you closely behind! Leaders reach out beyond their grasp. Leaders expand beyond their comfort zone or they will not grow. But if you reach out BEYOND your grasp and face fear head on by going to and BEYOND your limits, you will discover that your limits will grow.

120 to 139 Points: You have strong self-confidence but there is room for improvement. You know how to be a good leader and what it takes to be a great one. You inspire others to do all that you want them to do and yet make them feel good about it. As a strong leader you encourage others to be the best they can be and you convince others to have a great opinion of themselves. As a strong leader you make others believe that they can achieve whatever their goals are. You are also blessed with a knack of handling people and telling them exactly what they want to hear. Diplomacy is a card you play well. However, you must always remember to be humble and not to let overconfidence get the better of you. Work with what you have and show presence of mind when dealing with tricky situations or tricky people. Accept responsibility for what you do and take due credit for what you accomplish. Don't give up on what you start unless you have achieved all that you set out to achieve and more. Always focus on your vision for life. Remember—what is your vision in purpose? When you are passionate about what you want, your vision gets clearer and your actions are more refined and your leadership skills are sharpened. This is when you will have the potential to supercharge your business, your relationships, and your life. A vision without purpose is just a wish.

80 to 119 Points: Your leadership ability falls about midpoint. Your leadership qualities can be strengthened. As a leader, you strike a good balance between inspiring others and being inspired. You are a good leader but have the potential to be a great one. You have to realize your latent leadership qualities. Be confident, be responsible, be a people's person, be a leader. Learn to take things in your stride and improvise on what you have. Be goal-oriented and determined to achieve the target. What you must always remember is that leadership is more of a function of showing the way rather than being just a fancy title or position. You may sometimes suppress feelings in order to keep peace with others. Being honest and direct with others will raise relationships to a healthier level or it will release that relationship in your life. Either way, you win! You cannot control the reaction of others; you can only control your own reaction. Say what you want to say but say it in the way in which others want to hear it.

0 to 79 Points: You are more of a follower than a leader. You are more content with doing what people tell you to do rather than telling people what to do. You must be very good at what you do but you need someone to tell you what needs to be done. You are task oriented. You should learn to take initiative. Leadership is not something that one is born with. It has to be cultivated. Realize your own potential. Leadership is all about inspiring people. Focus on qualities that make you want to listen to a person and then try to imitate them in your own personality. But you must always remember that to inspire others to have confidence in you, you must first have confidence in yourself. In life, we get to choose our attitude...we can be defeated in whatever situation we find ourselves in OR we can choose to find the opportunity that is always available in every situation. Leaders throw themselves into the unknown. Leaders are willing to put themselves into challenging positions, so they are forced to rise to the challenge and move their lives toward success. Learn to rise to the occasion. In life, you only achieve what you focus on. See yourself as a powerful creator of your circumstances, and you will see opportunities to achieve your goals and dreams. Take the best out of what everyone in your group has to offer, add in your own ideas and see yourself leading others towards the stars!